So Far, So Good

SO FAR, SO GOOD

A Decade in Football

LIAM BRADY

Stanley Paul

London Melbourne Sydney Auckland Johannesburg

Stanley Paul & Co. Ltd

An imprint of the Hutchinson Publishing Group

3 Fitzroy Square, London W1P 6JD

Hutchinson Group (Australia) Pty Ltd
30–32 Cremorne Street, Richmond South, Victoria 3121
PO Box 151, Broadway, New South Wales 2007

Hutchinson Group (NZ) Ltd
32–34 View Road, PO Box 40–086, Glenfield, Auckland 10

Hutchinson Group (SA) (Pty) Ltd
PO Box 337, Bergvlei 2012, South Africa

First published 1980
© Liam Brady 1980

Set in Linotron Baskerville

Printed and bound in Great Britain by
REDWOOD BURN LIMITED
Trowbridge & Esher

ISBN 0 09 141790 2

Contents

Acknowledgements

I would like to record my thanks to Tony Roche for his invaluable help in writing this book; also to the following for allowing the use of copyright photographs: Colorsport, Danny Fox, K.R. Hailey, Stan McDonald, Newsport Press, Photosport, Sport and General, Sporting Pictures (UK) Ltd, Syndication International, Bob Thomas, P. Wardle.

Preface

You may wonder why I have written a book at such an early stage in my career. But this is not an autobiography of a twenty-four-year-old professional footballer.

I consider myself to be a very fortunate person. Football is my life and livelihood, as I wanted it to be from a very early age. But for every boy like me who makes the grade and succeeds in the game, many, many fail.

There are hundreds of reasons why a boy ends up on the soccer scrap-heap. I don't claim to know all of them, but I certainly know a lot. I have seen boys rejected, seen a close friend, whom I believed was probably better than me, turned down by Arsenal.

I came to terms with the harsh fact that the game is tough when it has to be, and that toughness is always revealed when the time comes to select the fortunate few from the hundreds of trialists.

There is very little room for sentiment, nor for soft words. People do not go out of their way to upset youngsters. But they do make it perfectly clear that whatever else they may become in life, it is not going to be a professional footballer, not at 'their' club anyway.

As I grew up and completed my apprenticeship I watched and listened and learned. Some of the things I saw were baffling, other situations upsetting and depressing. The game is something great, something very, very special. But it is also something which generates conflict and personality clashes.

The game is an enormous, living thing involving sport, money, business, showbusiness, the public, the press, radio and TV. From that lot it is only natural that personality clashes arise, people become a bit jealous or resentful if they think they are not paid enough, and so on.

All this can turn a youngster's head, shock him when he finds out that those larger-than-life football heroes he worshipped from afar as a schoolboy are really not as tall as they look from the terraces. That they are human, possess moods and tempers, personal strengths and weaknesses, have little fears and complexes just like the rest of the human race.

And that, on occasions, they can bite your head off for asking naïve questions if they are approached during a spell of personal problems.

I joined one of the biggest clubs in the world at a time when they had achieved the pinnacle of domestic success – the League Championship and FA Cup. The lesson I learned was that joining a successful club does not guarantee you a place in a successful team.

In my case, the club seemed to turn sour, bitter and unhappy as the months went by. I saw the two sides of mighty Arsenal – in trauma and triumph.

From all this I acquired an education nobody can give you. And any lad reading this book will still have to go through the whole process himself in order to cope with the profession.

But I hope to present a real-life picture of what it is like for a young lad leaving home to try his luck in the game.

I will point out the pitfalls and dangers, the avoidable mistakes. I will also tell my own story because, quite simply, it is comparable with many others and therefore has the value of being a good example of the way life in football really is.

From the very point where I gambled by not considering an alternative career, football has been a case of make-or-break for me.

I never wanted to do anything else. And I know there are hundreds of lads who feel the same way. All enthusiastic and more interested in playing than studying.

As I said, I consider myself fortunate . : . and in a good position to pass on a tip or two for the benefit of those lads starting out on the same unpredictable road I followed.

Forget the fact that I am twenty-four. I have experienced a

lot during my short time in the game.

I have always played in the First Division, appeared in successive Wembley Finals and walked off a loser and a winner, played in the UEFA Cup and the European Cup Winners' Cup and represented my country in European Championship and World Cup matches.

Make no mistake, I am still ambitious. But if an injury cut me down tomorrow I would not brood, nor would I feel sorry for myself. I have enjoyed so much in the game already and learned so much, about myself as well as others.

Believe me, when more than 40,000 people can openly comment on your job in public you get to know yourself very quickly.

You can feel lonely in the middle of a packed stadium and completely hemmed in by the presence of only one person. That's how football can get to you.

And get to you it does, like some kind of powerful drug. You can never get enough of it although it sometimes sets you up to be shot down in public.

Needless to say, I love every minute of the life. But then I have come to terms with the unpleasant things that happen, and any boy who fails to grow up overnight and stand on his own two feet cannot hope to succeed in the game.

In my case it's 'so far, so good'. And I want to help other lads to reach this stage by showing them how I handled – sometimes badly – my problems along the way. I'm also prepared to stand up and be counted when it comes to the controversial topics within the game, I hold a lot of strong views, and I am ready to air them.

1

Dublin to London

Expelled from school for captaining Ireland Schoolboys – that was the nightmare result of an honour most boys dream of, but which in my case led to confrontation, tears, the dread of not being able to sit my examinations, and unwanted newspaper headlines.

Yes, the first Liam Brady headline was controversial. But then what boy expects to be rejected and cold-shouldered for the 'crime' of being selected to represent his country?

The Brady household was still celebrating the news as I made my way to see my teachers at St Aidan's Christian Brothers School, Dublin. I thought my selection to skipper the Irish boys in Wales would be something they could be proud of.

Brother Walsh, the man in charge of school football, rarely showed emotion. He listened to my news, then told me it was nothing to do with him. I had to see the head brother. I don't know what I expected, but it certainly wasn't the reaction I got.

I suppose that at fifteen I was so full of excitement that the man's words took a little time to hit me. He told me that the school had a Gaelic challenge match against a team from Galway, which was scheduled for the same day as the Irish Schoolboys' game in Wales.

Now I can accept the importance of such games because they are all about old rivalry, prestige and inter-school competition. But I repeated that I had been chosen for my country and that I could not see any comparison between the two games.

I stood there, waiting for the fact to hit him and for the man to show that he was honoured and pleased for St Aidan's. But he looked straight at me and said: 'If you are not here on Saturday, then do not come into school on Monday. In fact don't come back again.'

I was more surprised and bewildered than anything else, but when I told my father he gave me the encouragement I needed. He told me not to worry and to go and do my very best for Ireland.

Well, I did what I believed to be right, played in Wales and came home with great memories. But by the time Sunday night edged into Monday morning, I realized that I was as scared as hell about going back to St Aidan's.

In the end I stayed at home and my father went up instead. He was just introducing himself to the head brother when the man snapped: 'Mr Brady, your boy is expelled. He is not to come back to this school.'

Then it really hit me. And I was very upset. My exams were coming up, and what about all my friends? But if I was upset, my father was absolutely fuming. He went to see a local priest and arranged for me to complete studies for my exams at another school – a local technical school. I had already explained that even if the brother changed his mind and allowed me back I would not have gone. It was a matter of principle and that brother had shown me his true colours.

Three days after the blow-up I saw the front page of the *Evening Herald* in Dublin with the headline blazing: CHRISTIAN BROTHER EXPELS BOY FOR PLAYING SOCCER.

On top of everything else I now thought I was the laughing stock of the city. I had a blazing row with my father and remember crying in frustration. It all seemed so stupid – to be picked for your country and end up in such a farcical mess for accepting!

Needless to say the brother in question was quoted in the paper denying ever saying any such thing. But all I knew was that I had to complete my studies and sit my exams. Nothing was more important at that time. Only now do I realize the value of the stand made by my father. It was important to let people know what was going on.

I went back to St Aidan's to sit my Intermediate Certificate examination – which thankfully went well – and that was the last time I went. I still think it is a pity because I enjoyed some great times there, and am convinced that those barbs were the actions of just one man and not the whole teaching staff.

Ironically a brother wrote to me years later and asked me if I minded them hanging one of my photographs in their hall of fame. I told him I would be honoured. And I am.

I am very pleased that my old school is proud of me after all. It would be a real shame if any bad feeling lingered on because of that one stupid incident with one stubborn man.

On the other hand, I owe that brother something he probably would not understand. He presented me with a bit of a crisis for a teenager to handle, and after the initial shock, I stuck to my guns.

Looking back, it was an important moment for me as an individual. For someone living outside Ireland it might be a bit difficult to understand, but attending a school where the Gaelic code is played meant problems if football openly conflicted with the popular sport.

I was not just bucking the system. I was taking on, or so it seemed at the time, a whole tradition. But it was my life and an important start to what I wanted my future to become. So I made my decision and faced the consequences.

Now I stick to the same attitude all the time. If I believe in something I will fight for it. That's not to say that I won't listen to reason, won't consider another person's point of view. But neither will I ever accept something blindly just because it happens to be scribbled on a piece of paper or presented to me as 'the way things are here'.

I believe that any young lad coming into the game needs to keep a clear head and think for himself. But then in my case my family always encouraged me to stand on my own two feet and voice my opinion – sensibly but also with conviction.

Country, family, friends, beliefs . . . all go to shape your life. In my case I come from a footballing family, born and bred in a city where the game reigns supreme and where I was provided with the opportunity of comparing League of Ireland football with the Football League from a very early age.

13

I was born on 13 February 1956 at number 12 Glenshesk Road, Whitehall, North Dublin, the seventh child of Edward and Eileen Brady.

Mine is an ordinary Irish family. My father is a docker, and although he was not a footballer he played and enjoyed the Gaelic code. The football in the Brady brothers stems from one Frank Brady – the Gaelic enthusiasts would call him the 'black sheep' – who was my father's uncle.

Frank played professional football for the now defunct Belfast Celtic and for a Cork team called Fordsons. He won two Irish caps during his time in Cork, both against Italy. The record books – and the family scrap books – show that he played in Turin on 21 March 1926 when Italy won 3–0, and in Dublin on 23 April 1927 when the Italians sneaked it 2–1.

Bradys were already playing football in Dublin before I was born. My brothers, Ray and Pat, were already beginning to show their capabilities by then, for the next member of the family to me is my brother Frank who is nine years my senior.

There were two girls in the family, but one died before I was born, leaving Breda sandwiched in between Pat and Ray, then Eamon, Frank and finally, me.

Pat and Ray went to play for Home Farm, one of the great breeding grounds for Irish players. Then Ray joined Transport, then members of the League of Ireland, and from there joined Millwall.

About one year later, Pat joined him at The Den. Queen's Park Rangers swooped to sign Ray . . . and Pat rejoined his brother again, this time at Loftus Road.

By 1963, Ray was an international defender and made his debut for Ireland in their European Nations Cup tie with Austria in Vienna on 25 September of that year. The 0–0 draw guaranteed a big gate for the return, and sure enough, Ireland beat Austria 3–2 in Dublin, Ray playing his part, and I was there to cheer him.

Watching your country play is always an exciting experience. But in my case the emotions were much stronger than that. Out there was my brother, a member of my family, a Brady.

I felt like yelling the fact to the rest of the crowd. But I was

14

too numb, too anxious, hoping Ray would do well. It is very difficult to remember all of the things that went through my mind that day. I was only seven. But I was very aware that it was a special occasion for the whole family.

It would be stretching things a bit too far to suggest that Ray's performance and my being there on the day actually fired my ambitions to follow in his footsteps. But on the other hand the football atmosphere within our family was a very strong one. And I have no doubt that seeing Ray playing for Ireland did make a big impression. The difficulty lies in pin-pointing the impression at that time.

I think it is natural for a boy to want to copy his big brothers in a lot of ways. Everyone in your family influences you as you grow up. So with all the talk about football and all the questions school-friends asked concerning my brothers, it just seemed natural for me to want to become a footballer.

Ray went on to win six full caps, so naturally, with so much experience in the family, I have always known that there are very few football problems facing me that have not already faced my brothers. It is a different era, yes. But it is still the pro-fessional game.

The problem of employment and security has been as big a problem in Dublin as it is in every major city. I grew up know-ing that the working man depends on his good health and his boss to keep the roof over the head of his family.

That is the down-to-earth reality of working life, no matter what your job. It applies to me and every other player as much as it applies to the fans when they are earning their bread. An injury can end your playing career. An injury can stop a docker from doing his job.

I believe that my brother Eamon was a good player. But he decided to take up a career in Irish shipping, and went to sea where he did well and won various promotions in rank.

Frank took the familiar route to Home Farm before going to Shamrock Rovers as a professional. After a spell working in Australia, he came back to Dublin and is playing for Home Farm again, now members of the League of Ireland.

So the fact that I had my heart set on the game is hardly sur-prising.

15

I began my education at Larkhill Primary School, and even then football was the one sport all the boys wanted to play. We played Gaelic football at school, however, and I genuinely enjoyed it. I enjoy playing any sport.

By the time I moved on to St Aidan's I was already playing football for St Kevin's Boys' Club, one of countless boys' football clubs in Dublin. At school you played Gaelic games, but outside it was football.

I first experienced organized football when I was nine and continued playing while completing my education. The game is, among other things, a great medium of expression. And with every game I knew that nothing else gripped my imagination as much, nothing could stimulate me in the same way.

Arsenal entered my life when I was thirteen, in the shape of Mr Malwyn Roberts, a senior scout from North Wales. He teamed up with the club's Dublin scout, Mr Bill Darby and watched one of my games for St Kevin's. So at thirteen I was invited to Highbury for trials . . . but more about that later.

Suffice to say that my game was developing along lines that I hoped would lead me across the Irish Sea and into one of the Football League teams which I used to watch with such fascination and admiration on *Match of the Day*.

You see, to so many of us, England was where the game was played at the top level. We admired and respected our own League football, but common sense told us that the game in England was the big-time, the place to be as a professional.

The majority of my school-pals watched a League of Ireland team, but openly supported – albeit from afar – either Liverpool or Manchester United, Celtic or Everton or one of the top British clubs.

I was the exception. I followed the great players, not their teams. I took an interest in individuals, especially when they were playing at their best. I loved the glamour and the colour, the skill and excitement.

At ten I remember the Manchester United of George Best, Denis Law and Bobby Charlton. All top-class players and all magical in their own right. I quite happily latched on to one name at a time and would go out and be him when playing in a Dublin park.

16

I remember Rodney Marsh playing for QPR in the 1967 League Cup Final – the first at Wembley – and how he scored a marvellous individual goal in their 3–2 win over West Brom. So, for weeks after I was a Marsh fanatic. He will never know how many games he played for St Kevin's Boys' Club!

Then came my appreciation of Leeds United and of John Giles. By the time I reached 1970 I was involved with Arsenal, so I made sure that I 'was' an Arsenal star when I played.

The point is that every week I was someone different. Not a man in a certain club's colours, but an individual of skiil and style. That is what I admired and that is what I wanted to become. I was – and still am – a tremendous admirer of the individual and his skills.

Living in England means that you have the game at your fingertips. Nip down the road, or catch a bus or train, and you can stand and watch some of Europe's best players from a few yards. In Dublin we couldn't do that.

When I was at school, like all the football fanatics of Dublin, I had to make do with reading the papers and magazines and, when it arrived, watching the television.

I still remember the first family to get a television set in our road. They were great because we would all crowd into their front room to watch *Match of the Day* on Saturday night, go home and dream of what we'd seen, then go out on Sunday and become great stars (in our imagination).

And we had some very good players, even at that age. I was fortunate in that St Kevin's was one of the best teams around. We won lots of competitions and were certainly the city's top team of its age group. I suppose most of us had the same dream – to become a professional.

Sometimes I think that the dividing line between the dream and the reality is amazingly slender. Certainly I know one player who I believed would go all the way to England, yet when the chance came, it went wrong for him.

Pat Daly and I were great mates at St Kevin's. Without blowing a trumpet, we were the two best players in the team and to this day I believe that there was very little to choose between us.

I admired his skill and his timing and his vision. We played

17

well together and were definitely on the same wavelength. So, jumping forward again for a moment, when I was fourteen and involved with Arsenal for a year, they invited Pat over for trials.

They even asked me for my opinion. Unfortunately, at fourteen you don't always come across as definitely as you can when you grow older, but I believed in Pat and he obviously did enough to warrant being asked over.

But on the day he froze and did not make an impression. Yet I know he had the ability. Perhaps the system is a bit too tough. Youngsters are just pitched into a situation that is so crucial to their whole lives, lining up with total strangers and in a foreign country, wanting to do everything at once to make a good impression. Believe me, those trials can be an ordeal. More of that later, also.

Pat went home to Dublin and played professional for Shelbourne. Now he is back at St Kevin's, helping boys on their way in the game. God alone knows how many more boys there are who could, perhaps, make an impression in the game, given a certain set of circumstances. It is not *all* about skill and natural ability.

Hundreds of skilful boys never make it; hundreds of less skilful artisans do.

My circumstances certainly helped: brothers in the game with experience and a close-knit family unit always there to support and encourage, along with a passion for the game burning inside, while still unfamiliar with the occasional bucket of cold water threatening to douse those flames.

Growing up in Dublin meant a low-key, but nevertheless real, anti-English feeling. It is natural. The school books, the history, the years of troubles and the tales, told and re-told, of one scrap after another between the countries.

But not even politics, nor history, mattered as much to me as football. If someone had asked me to go to Germany or Holland to play football I would have turned them down flat. But England? That was different. That was class, the very best in the game as I knew it.

England, however was a foreign land, a place where, I was told by my friends, it was usually raining and none too

18

friendly. Not like home.

Living in Dublin means living in a community. People know you. They want to know you. In many ways you are all the same type of people. But London, as I discovered later, for all its attractions and size, is a terribly lonely place. You can live next door to a family and they don't even introduce themselves.

On the other hand, once you have lived in London, to go home and realize just what little privacy you had in Dublin is to discover that you really want a happy medium — communication and friendship as well as a private life.

Dublin and London represent the extremes.

But on the football front, Dublin compares more with Liverpool. In both cities the people have a craving for the game, a real need to be involved in it, to play it, discuss it, read about it, dream about it. The big difference is, of course, Dublin does not have the same quality of team.

Yet if you took the time to list the number of players who have been discovered in Dublin and have gone on to make the grade in the Football League, the only word that would adequately describe your findings would be phenomenal.

Such was the background that prepared me for Highbury and the beginning of a career that seemed to turn horribly sour before it ever began.

That fateful day when Malwyn Roberts and Bill Darby singled me out of the twenty-two players was obviously the most important of my schooldays.

They went straight to my home. My mother answered the door, listened to their invitation to take her youngest son to England . . . and told them to come back the next day when my father was in.

The next day I made sure I was out. Having spoken to them after that game I knew what it was all about, but I did not want to be sitting there gaping at them while listening to the news I had dreamed of hearing.

My father always had the opinion that his children should have the right to make up their own minds about what they wanted to do. Accepting that such freedom has limits it allowed us to stand on our own two feet from an early age and express our opinions.

So he told the Arsenal scouts that if I wanted to go, I was free to do so. My first visit to England started badly. The trial – the moment I had thought of day and night from the moment Malwyn Roberts first spoke to me – began like some kind of nightmare.

For thirty agonizing minutes I could not put a foot right. And, although I did not know it at the time, Mr Roberts was close to grabbing a shovel and digging himself a hole in which to hide.

Fortunately I settled down after that half-hour and made some kind of reasonable impression. Just as well! Because to this day, whenever I see Mr Roberts he reminds me of how I mortified him. What I did not know was that he told Arsenal he had unearthed 'a real little Irish gem'.

Arsenal followed up their interest and I came over to England for short stays, to train, show my paces and let the club see how I was progressing. But all the time I was studying at St Aidan's, determined to get those exams.

The expulsion shook me a bit and, as I said, the publicity was the last thing I wanted. But the thing that really hit me hard was when the time came to leave Ireland to join Arsenal full-time.

Up to then the whole thing had seemed a great adventure, leaving home for two or three weeks at a time. Just like a series of holidays. But you always go home after a holiday and I suddenly became aware of the fact that I had to say goodbye to friends I'd grown up with and leave my family.

At fifteen it felt as if I was going to the other side of the world and never coming back.

I wonder how many boys feel this way when the time comes to kiss their mums and shake hands with their dads before taking their first step on the road to a career as a professional.

Probably all the boys leave their homes as I left mine, gripping a suitcase as tightly as I gripped mine, gritting their teeth against the welling tears and making a great show of bravado to disguise the nerves deep in their stomachs and the sadness of the wrench away from the security of home.

Every season comes a new batch, from all corners of Britain and Ireland, endowed with a variety of talents and convinced that each is the answer to the game's lack of individual talent.

The harsh reality is that the vast majority never make the grade.

I did make the grade. But this is not a boast. No, I am truly grateful because I have seen many lads trudging away from the game, puzzled at the rejection that has shattered all their dreams, worried about their futures, the limited job prospects, the reality of facing their friends who all believed they were going to oust some Denis Law or George Best from his pedestal.

And because I made the grade does not mean that things all fell nicely into place. They did not. I had problems along the way, thoughts of packing it all up and going home, worries about my game not progressing.

I have experienced just about all the things today's youngster faces when he begins his apprenticeship.

Ahead are days of incredible excitement, stimulation, the feeling of personal achievement and pride in self-expression.

But there are also tough times, pitfalls, black days, moments of acute loneliness, frustration, nagging doubts about your ability, the possibility of injury ruining all your plans, touches of homesickness and even boredom.

It is the greatest profession in the world. It is also one of the most demanding.

And it was the attraction of the game, the sheer magnetism of it, that helped me to walk away from Dublin.

Little did I know what lay in store – the feeling of bitter disappointment that steadily grew until I returned to Ireland for Christmas . . . and told my family I was never going back.

2

Apprenticeship and Other Traumas

Disillusioned, disappointed and determined never to go back, I left Arsenal in December 1971 and went home to Dublin.

It seemed as if all my dreams had been shattered during six months of cleaning boots, clearing out dressing rooms, setting up props for the senior players' training sessions and enduring increasing criticism about the way I was playing.

I was still two months from my sixteenth birthday and, as soon as I was re-united with my family, it hit me just how much I had missed them and everyone else I knew. Wild horses were not going to drag me back to London. Professional football, and all its regimentation, could go to hell.

That is how close I came to missing out on a life that shows you the world, makes you grow up quickly, gives you a tremendous sense of purpose and achievement and helps you to shoulder and cope with responsibility.

And that is how close hundreds of boys come to turning their backs on the game. Some actually do. It proves too much for them too soon. Confrontation with professional football, and all it entails and demands, knocks the wind from their lungs and makes them long for the comfort of family and home.

My advice to any boy given the opportunity of a football apprenticeship is to come to terms with a new way of life and knuckle down to learning what is, after all, a profession. No matter what job you take up you have to learn the ropes from scratch.

In my case I was convinced that I had made up my mind. And when I was ten days late reporting back to Highbury, the letters started arriving. Naturally, Arsenal wanted to know what was wrong, what was I doing?

I wrote back, explaining my feelings. But no sooner had I done so than I began to miss the very atmosphere that two weeks earlier I could not wait to escape!

My return to the club was my own decision. I discovered that even those tasks I disliked were part of my education and I wanted to make it to the top.

So what was the problem in the first place? Well it was simply that I was not prepared for the way of life I had chosen and discovered that I knew little about the workings of a professional football club.

When I first arrived at Highbury in the summer of 1971 I walked into a club still echoing the celebrations of their League Championship and FA Cup 'double' of a few months earlier.

I came with six other apprentices, lads I'd already met during the brief visits to England, when I was getting to know the club and the area. We teamed up with nine apprentices already at Highbury creating a mini-squad of sixteen.

At the time of writing there are only two of us left at Arsenal, Ritchie Powling and me. Some of the others joined other clubs, some went non-League . . . the majority never made it at all.

That statistic in itself tells a tale. We all came with the same ambition, to become good professionals. But for every one boy who goes on and makes the grade, a hell of a lot fail. It is a fact of football life, and one to be faced from the outset.

The last thing a boy should have is a negative attitude towards himself or his chances. But optimism must go hand in hand with realism. There is no comparison between football as you know it and play it for fun and football as you play it for a living.

This discovery shocked me. I needed to go away from the whole scene to get things into perspective. But once I had made up my mind and made my own decision, I quickly came to terms with the job.

The arrival of the new apprentices that summer was just one more change in the already vastly altered set-up.

Don Howe, so instrumental in the creation of that great 'double' team, went to The Hawthorns to manage West Bromwich Albion. With him went the youth team coach, Brian

Whitehouse. That meant that we began our careers with a youth-team coach, Ian Crawford, who was also new to the scene.

Dave Smith was appointed Reserve-team coach and Steve Burtenshaw became first-team coach. The club was going through a big transition.

Leaving home is a traumatic experience. That's why it is very important for a boy to move into friendly, homely digs. I was fortunate in that I met a family – Mr and Mrs Rowland – on one of my trial stays at Highbury, and I asked to be allowed to stay with them. They treated me tremendously and they lived only five minutes away from the ground.

Thanks to them I never really felt so homesick that I had to grab my bag and run to Heathrow. Obviously I missed my folks, but Mr and Mrs Rowland made me feel really at home. And take my word for it, that counts for a hell of a lot, especially when you are fifteen or sixteen, and hundreds of miles from home.

On my first day as an apprentice I turned up at 9.00 a.m. on the Monday morning and by lunch time I was totally aware of how much I had to learn. As the first few days passed I tried to adjust.

The sheer professionalism of the place amazed me. We were treated like a junior version of the first team. The professional approach went all the way down through the teams, and for the first time I experienced pre-match meals, training at set times, strictness in so many aspects of the life including what time you went to bed, what time you got up. We were being groomed for the future.

Apprentices are always at the beck and call of the seniors. So we knew what was in store for us the moment we arrived for work on Monday.

Our first job was to load the kit and equipment on to the coach for training. Then we laid out the kit for the first-team lads and while they were getting changed we had to fetch and carry the training props on their behalf.

This I enjoyed – most of us did. It meant contact with the seniors and they were where we all wanted to go – the top.

Then we would begin our training. At that early part of the

season, the beginning of July, the work was geared to getting us fit – stamina work, long-distance runs, circuit training. It was bloody exhausting, especially when you are totally new to it.

Most boys who experience this necessary beginning will find themselves throwing up in a bush en route, hoping not to be spotted. What they won't realize is that the seniors suffer the very same reaction to tough training when it begins at the start of a new season. It's something of a shock to the system – even a tuned-up system.

The joy at the end of it all, of course, was actually playing. That was all I ever wanted to do, get a ball and play. But most of the week was all about hard work – learning, grafting and mopping up after the first teamers.

Friday was the favourite day because it was pay day. We would collect our £6, count it, count it again, then go back to the daily chores. Being the day before match day we had to clean out the dressing rooms. And it did not matter who was playing at home – first team or reserves.

On Saturday we played in the South East Counties League. And once again the professional approach was very impressive. It always makes an impact on young lads.

We would board a coach and travel to play names like Tottenham Hotspur or Chelsea. Never mind that they were the same age group as us. We wore the club's shirts and were representatives of Arsenal.

Make no mistake, that pride comes through, even at fifteen. Our side was a good one. Our squad was a good one. Yet the lads who made the grade can be counted on one hand.

John Matthews played a number of senior games, but was transferred to Sheffield United. The same applied to Brian Hornsby who moved on to Peterborough and later Sheffield Wednesday. Dave Donaldson joined Millwall and Barrie Vassallo moved to Plymouth Argyle.

As I said earlier, that left Ritchie Powling and me at Arsenal. Frank Stapleton joined us later, but from the original bunch the majority never made it in the game.

Because of his age, the apprentice is vulnerable. He is unaware of adult levels of thought and reasoning. He is used to school, family, football for fun. And even when told what life is all about, he will often fret and worry when things go wrong.

Now I have never been a great one for rules and regulations. So when I began to think that I was not making any progress as a player, I became depressed with the whole business.

The professional game gradually cheesed me off, the chores became a bore and the constant pressure of discipline and graft highlighted to me that I seemed to be doing more of everything except what I thought I came over to do . . . play football.

I was not very big, nor very strong. Unlike the majority of apprentices, who look big and strong and therefore often look better than they are, I was trailing in the muscles department.

Then my game dipped. I began having a bad time. They got on at me more and more and this criticism, day after day, was something else I was not used to.

One of the things an apprentice must accept is that most of his ideas about the game are knocked sideways once he begins learning how to become a professional.

Like every lad who ever kicked a ball, I had my own likes and dislikes. I am a player who wants the ball as much as possible. I enjoy having possession. And as a youngster, I disliked parting with it more than was absolutely necessary.

That may be fine when playing park football. But at club-apprentice level you are introduced to discipline, organization, team-work, unselfishness, when to hold the ball and when to release it.

Coupled with my lack of muscles, my initial difficulty in coming to terms with playing football the way Ian Crawford wanted me to play led to some poor personal displays. Looking back, the criticism was necessary and good for me. But as a teenager I became sensitive about the situation and began to think it was personal.

I did not rebel. But I did dig in my heels just a little. I resented the fact that strength and weight were such an advantage for the other lads. I was knocked off the ball too easily and sometimes crowded out because I held on to the ball too long.

I wanted to show them that I could play. I really wanted to make an impression and prove that I was able to overcome my size through my ability.

The thing that hit me hardest, however, was being accused

26

of deliberately flunking out of an important game.

Shortly before the Christmas holidays we were scheduled to play a vital Southern Junior Floodlit Cup tie at Highbury. Now, believe me, we rarely got the chance of playing at the ground, so it was something to look forward to, a real thrill.

It was winter and I developed a lousy cold. So when it came to the game I had to drop out. I felt ill and disappointed. So when I heard the accusation it hit me hard that they could even think like that.

So I went home. After six days in Dublin it came to the day of reckoning, time to go back. I told my mother I was not going.

When I did go back to Arsenal I found that, if anything, they went a bit easier on me and certainly never made a fuss of the fact that I was so late back to work!

But I made up for it. Things began to slot into place and I improved my game and made the progress the club hoped I would make.

February brought my sixteenth birthday and soon after I was selected to play for the Reserves. Once again this meant the contact with some first-team players, a vitally important part of an apprentice's education.

That season, 1971–72, I was in and out of the Reserves and played mainly for the South East Counties team. But those few games in the Football Combination were all about playing in the same team as George Armstrong or Peter Marinello – they seemed to have spells in the first team alternately – Charlie George, George Graham and even Frank McLintock.

Frank went through a bad spell and Jeff Blockley was in at centre-half. For me that bad spell was a godsend. And it brought home to me that apprentices are not simply thrown in at the deep end. Selection is carefully planned so that they have experienced players with them on the field, men who can help and advise and apply a calming hand.

You come across good and bad attitudes in all walks of life. Football is no different. So no apprentice need feel shocked when he turns out for the Reserves and finds that some of the 'dropped' first-teamers he has looked forward to playing alongside reveal that they believe the whole situation is beneath their dignity.

27

Oh yes, one or two will give a lousy example to the very youngsters they should shine for, the very lads who probably admire them greatly and hope to be like them.

These are the seniors who moan, stroll and generally gripe about being relegated to the 'stiffs' instead of fighting hard to regain their first-team place. They exist, at every club.

But in the vast majority of clubs, so do the others who go out of their way to give a good example and take the trouble to listen to problems and give advice.

They are often sharp, abrupt and demanding. But they also make you feel an equal and give you great confidence.

That is what Frank McLintock did for me. He was, in a word, fantastic. I loved every minute of those Reserve games because he pointed out my mistakes and gave me sound advice.

George Graham did the same thing, for my benefit and the benefit of other boys. He would make a point of telling you what was right. This is all part of the apprentice's learning process.

But he must be careful not to note the example of the players who don't try, who sulk and make it obvious that they don't want to play.

The player who had the biggest influence on me was Alan Ball. He always took a genuine interest in the progress of the kids anyway because he is, by nature, totally wrapped up in football. But he seemed to single me out for special attention.

Often he would just talk to me, asking how we got on, who scored, how did I play, what was I good at and what had I done that was not so clever.

It was an important kind of contact that meant the world to me at sixteen. Here was this world-class international, a World Cup winner and League Championship winner taking the time to discuss the game with a sixteen-year-old hopeful from Dublin.

And when you realize that some of the senior players would hardly say good morning to you, 'Bally's' interest and advice were priceless.

I remember big John Radford, on the outside a dour Yorkshireman with little to say to his team-mates, never mind the apprentices, being just about audible on the

28

few occasions I had the nerve to say 'morning John' when passing him in the corridor.

Yet when I played in the first team with John later we became genuine friends. He is a deep character, sincere and the possessor of a dry humour. But to strangers he always seemed a bit daunting. The apprentices had the same opinion.

Bob Wilson, one of the bravest goalkeepers I have seen, always seemed aloof when I was an apprentice. I never knew how to approach him and so I rarely did. But once again, when I got to know him, 'Willow' was revealed to be a real student of his profession, a man who wrote a thesis on goalkeeping at teachers' training college and later wrote his own book on the subject.

This was for me – and is for every apprentice – the magic of it all, the rubbing of shoulders in corridors, dressing rooms and, occasionally, in the Reserves with the stars.

I have already explained that individuals, rather than teams, grabbed my imagination. So Charlie George was the player who, along with 'Bally', made the biggest impression on me.

The crowd adored Charlie because he comes from that part of North London and used to stand on the North Bank supporting Arsenal as a kid. The apprentices adored him as well. He oozed class, skill and confidence. He was the king-pin of the team on his day.

But sadly it was around that time that Charlie became disillusioned with the club, and when I believe his game began to slide. It's difficult to pinpoint these things specifically, but he had something special to offer and it did not shine through as often as it should have.

Being realistic, very few boys – if any ever again – are likely to begin their apprenticeships with a club still warm from the glow of a 'double'.

As you can imagine, Arsenal was the place to be then and at times you thought the Reserve team could have held its own in the League!

For me it was a marvellous education, watching the result of success, the effect it has on a club, the players and fans and how, like a drug, it has to be provided in regular doses.

When a club enjoys a successful period, everyone connected with that club reflects the fact.

Supporters enjoy Monday mornings when they can face their workmates with heads held high and describe their club's most recent triumph. They enjoy going to their pub or club for the same reasons, and willingly enter conversations about football because they know that they are involved in a successful scene.

Players walk with a spring in their step. They become all too willing to attend public functions, face reporters, look straight into a television camera lens or stand for ages signing autographs. I am not saying that unsuccessful teams go into hiding or shun the world. Far from it. It is just that you can see how much more the player from the winning team enjoys recognition.

This is how it was at Arsenal. And because the senior players were on top of the world – at least they were there before I joined and just beginning to descend when I did arrive – their confidence and sense of well-being spread throughout the ranks, all the way down to the apprentices.

But only when things begin to change and success is gradually discussed in the past tense, do you see the other side of the coin.

Success is a drug. Some clubs experience it once and spend years trying to find it again. But the likes of Arsenal, Liverpool, Spurs, Manchester United and the other top clubs enjoy regular doses.

The trouble lies in this very fact. Because, while the club with the single moment of treasured glory can still enjoy a solid existence afterwards, the top club suffers visible withdrawal symptoms if the gaps between doses are too long.

Supporters, accustomed to success, grow impatient and are prone to making unfavourable comparisons between the existing side and the last successful side. Sometimes a touch of panic sets in as a club attempts to recapture golden days with a large influx of new players, because it does not always follow that the eleven best individual players will make the best team.

Highbury was hooked on the drug of success. And there can be little doubt the troubles within the club in the seasons after the 'double' were largely a result of withdrawal symptoms.

I suppose this is where fate plays a part. Before Arsenal approached me I discovered that Coventry City were interested and, like so many Dublin lads, I had a personal liking for the scene at Old Trafford where so many Irish players find a second home.

They were not my team as such, and when interest was expressed I had already made up my mind to join Arsenal.

That season saw Arsenal back at Wembley where they lost the Centenary Final 1–0 to Leeds, Allan Clarke delivering the killer blow with a second-half header.

Such was the impact of the previous season that many fans actually considered losing at Wembley to be some kind of failure, forgetting, of course, that getting there even once is more than most League clubs have achieved in their history. And some such histories go back more than a century.

Around this time a tall, dark-haired fifteen-year-old arrived from Dublin as an apprentice and teamed up with us. He was shy and talented, a boy named Frank Stapleton with whom I was destined to share Wembley misery and joy, and international failure and success.

With so much happening at Highbury the season and the summer slid by while I continued to learn my job. I was selected to play two games for Ireland's youth team, another great honour, and when I reached seventeen Arsenal made their decision concerning my future.

To my absolute delight they offered me a two-year contract at £20 a week and I walked out into Avenall Road a fully-fledged professional footballer.

The money and contract gave me confidence, security and breathing space. Now I had two whole years more with the club for certain, and even at seventeen that meant a lot.

My apprenticeship was over. But what did I learn from it?

I learned that football as a profession makes a man of a boy more quickly than most other professions. That without discipline you cannot hope to succeed – as a player or indeed in any walk of life. That criticism is more than just an attack of a personal nature. Often it is helpful and important in the development of your career.

31

I do not believe that you should accept all criticism without reply. But I do believe that without it, you cannot improve. If nobody bothers to help you to become a better player, then you will not be criticized, but neither will you learn very much.

I learned that no one player is bigger than his club, nor his team. Every single player is replaceable. Certainly in the eyes of his employers he is.

You must be honest with yourself and your club. Any attempt to cut corners in your work or your training will be reflected as your career develops . . . most probably as a weakness.

I learned that football is a game which you never stop learning about. And the best players and managers in the world are agreed on this. I have heard many men say that they were still learning about their profession even as they prepared to retire.

I advise every boy entering the game to listen to every scrap of advice given, chew it over, see what works for you as an individual and disregard the rest.

It is all too easy to overwhelm a youngster with waffle and jargon. My belief in the individual is strong. So stand on your own two feet, make decisions for yourself, never forgetting to listen to all that advice because, from every dose you get, something will prove invaluable.

But don't feel duty-bound to swallow and agree with everything thrown your way. You have a mind and talent all of your own. Use them!

3

Highs and Lows at Highbury

Dressing-room rows and friction, a personal confrontation with manager Bertie Mee, a triumphant League debut followed by a painful crash back down to earth, and a tragic double injury to the man who tried more than most to help me, resulting in the supreme irony – an extended run in the First Division for me.

Enough ingredients there to span a player's entire career. But in my case they proved to be a series of events which occurred while I was trying to make some kind of impression at Highbury.

The sign of a club's greatness must be its ability to keep up appearances for the benefit of the fans and the media, even when things behind the scenes are far from good.

Such was the case at Arsenal. I doubt if many people knew of the unhappiness creeping through the corridors as the great 'double' team began to break up – and in some controversial circumstances, be broken up.

I suppose the problem with success is that it has to be sustained. Look at the absolute drivel directed at Liverpool if they allow their standards to slip to such appalling depths as dropping a home point or losing one away game.

One of the truly great clubs in the history of the game has set such high standards that it is now judged by those standards and not by the standards by which the rest of us are measured.

The Arsenal squad of 1972–73 was still largely made up of players who had won the Inter Cities Fairs Cup in 1970, the League Championship and FA Cup in 1971 and finished FA Cup runners-up in 1972. Odd as it may sound, there arises a definite problem of motivation. Players discover that the very most they can achieve will only equal what they have already achieved – and the chances of them doing so are so remote that even gambling addicts would not bother.

Arsenal's 'double' came a decade after Tottenham Hotspur's, and before that . . . well I doubt if any playing members of the Aston Villa 'double' winners were around to see their feat repeated by Bill Nicholson's Spurs – because Villa had won the 'double' in 1897! That's how long it took to repeat.

Faced with this problem, Arsenal needed an injection of new ideas and new blood. But there was also a hell of a lot to be said for keeping together such an experienced and gifted bunch of professionals.

Plugging away in the Reserves, I knew that the club believed that I had a chance of making the grade. With me at this level were Brian Hornsby, Brendan Batson and David Price. We worked hard, week after week, hoping for that breakthrough, that chance to show what we could really do in front of a big crowd.

When you are so keen and aware of every selection pinned on the board, you also become tuned into the very atmosphere of a club. And you notice the negative as well as positive vibrations.

One of the obvious problems was also very understandable. Don Howe's move to manage West Bromwich Albion disappointed many of the senior players. Under his particular brand of coaching they had reached for the stars and touched them. But already those stars were obscured by darkening clouds.

The fans realized that the team was going through a major transition. But what they didn't know was that feelings were coming to a head amongst the players.

Not all the seniors could see eye-to-eye with Steve Burtenshaw who, as first-team coach, was faced with the unenviable job of following a man who had won everything.

It must have been very difficult for Burtenshaw. I did not have that much to do with him because he was working with the senior players, but it was obvious that the players were disappointed that Don Howe had left and resented the fact that the club let him go.

Burtenshaw faced the awesome task of maintaining

Arsenal's remarkable level of success – in itself an almost impossible job – knowing all the while that the very best he could ever achieve would only be compared with Howe's achievements and therefore lose some of its value.

Yet the team was playing very well. Alan Ball, George Armstrong, John Radford, Ray Kennedy, Eddie Kelly – they were still knitting together well, still maintaining their reputations as one of the best outfits in Britain.

What the fans do not see, of course, is the gradual feeling of disillusionment that follows personality clashes. Charlie George and Bertie Mee did not see things the same way, and quite honestly, Charlie hovered between the substitute's bench, the Reserves and the first team. It all seemed such a waste of talent.

Frank McLintock began to realize that Jeff Blockley was destined to become his successor despite the fact that the majority of the lads believed Frank to be the best skipper in the League and capable of doing a first-rate job in the team.

George Graham had already joined Manchester United, another part of the team gone. Graham was a key member of the great Arsenal side.

I saw this happening. But it was none of my business and I kept my nose out of things. It was difficult enough to keep my own game improving at the rate Reserve-team manager Dave Smith demanded.

I was still too slight of build. So while the rest of the lads had their weight to add to their game, I was forced to rely purely on my ability with the ball. In many ways this proved to be for the good. But Dave became a little anxious about the absence of fat on my frame and I had to go on a planned diet – to build me up. I swallowed endless helpings of Complan, iron-based foods and traditional body-building meals.

As I said, in February 1973, I was offered a two-year contract. At last I could see some light at the end of the tunnel. To an outsider, such a moment probably seems unimportant, something a player simply expects. But that is not the case. You think about your chances every week. You hope to God you are going to be given that chance. You dread the hand on the shoulder, the chilling words

35

that spell the end of your hopes and dreams.

But for all my joy at being taken on, I was quickly made aware that I had a lot of work still to do, even in the Reserves. My game was developing and Dave Smith was pleased with my progress.

Not that I lacked encouragement. Smith was aware of my anxiety and let me see that I was progressing by combining criticism with praise.

But then Smith was more than used to working with players at this level. He was chief coach at Sheffield Wednesday, and at Newcastle United when they won the Inter Cities Fairs Cup in 1969 before joining Arsenal in 1971.

He put me through my paces and made it clear that the only way to break into the first team was hard work followed by more hard work and dedication.

I was not surprised when Dave Smith decided to accept the challenge of becoming a manager. He took over at Mansfield in 1974 and two years later became number one at Southend United.

Slowly but surely I became aware of a greater consistency in my play. I knew I had a long, hard slog ahead of me. But it was heartening to gain confidence after some good displays for the Reserves.

But when it came to the thing that mattered most – playing in the first team – Brendan Batson, Brian Hornsby and David Price all made it before me.

Just when I got the news that Arsenal wanted me to stay, Brendan was selected to play against West Bromwich Albion at The Hawthorns on 28 February, 1973. The game ended 0–0 but for Brendan the great news was that he was in again the following week, 3 March, against Sheffield United when he collected his first League win bonus as Arsenal won 3–2.

Me, I swallowed more Complan and gritted my teeth, determined to be next. But it was not to be.

As the season drew to a close, disaster struck. Second Division Sunderland beat Arsenal 2–1 in the FA Cup semi-final at Hillsborough, Sheffield. The fact that Bob Stokoe's lads went on to beat Leeds 1–0 in the final meant nothing to the Highbury fans.

Yet Arsenal finished League runners-up that season, a great achievement under any circumstances. But if the fans were a bit disappointed, the players were openly disgruntled.

For the last game of the season, away to Leeds United, changes had to be made because of injuries. It was good to see more young players getting into the first team. Brian Hornsby wore the number 11 shirt on that 9 May . . . and when he was taken off in a 6–1 mauling, David Price went on as substitute.

How much more bloody Complan?

The expected changes took place. Steve Burtenshaw left and was replaced by Bobby Campbell. But the real bombshell of the beginning of season 1973–74 was the transfer of Frank McLintock to London neighbours, Queen's Park Rangers.

Few of the senior players could understand this decision to part with so valuable and experienced a pro as Frank. He made 312 League appearances for the club, helped youngsters such as me more than anybody realized and provided a level of leadership, on and off the pitch, that few players can give.

To make matters worse, Arsenal made a woeful start to the season. The fans were puzzled and the players unhappy. Losing 2–0 at home to Leicester City on 8 September left Arsenal twentieth in the First Division table – an unheard-of situation.

And it was then that Bertie Mee and Bobby Campbell decided that changes had to be made. A new team had to be built, slowly and carefully, and I could sense the mood around the club.

For me it was a very special season. Because I arrived for pre-season training, not as a hopeful apprentice facing boot and baggage chores, but as a professional approaching another make-or-break stage of my life. I really wanted to make it quickly, to make things happen for myself. And I knew that the only way to do that was to achieve a level of consistency with the Reserves that would have to be noticed.

I had come through the learning-the-ropes spell. The seniors, such as McLintock and Graham, had helped me to harden my approach to the game, to give as good as I got and lose the feeling of being a little bit overawed in the presence of top-class opponents.

This is a very important hurdle to overcome. There is always the feeling of being slightly inferior to an opponent who, for example, is playing in the Reserves after being dropped from his first team or while recovering from an injury. But what players fail to appreciate is that a senior, fighting his way back towards first-team recognition, is just as worried about a young opponent, because he knows he is expected to come out on top and worries about an apprentice or a fresh young pro showing him up.

My advice to a lad in this situation is to stick your chest out, get your head up and show what you can do. Nobody can ever do better than his best, and not every man gives his best all the time, so the more often you achieve this type of consistency the quicker your career will move along at a good, encouraging pace.

And at the end of it all, if you are destined to make the grade, comes the moment you have dreamed of night after night – playing in the Football League.

No matter what success you achieve throughout your career, the date of your League debut – and all the circumstances which surrounded it – will stick in your memory. It certainly sticks in mine.

The turning point in my career was the visit of Tranmere Rovers to Highbury for a Football League Cup second-round tie. Despite all the usual newspaper talk of giant-killing, Arsenal were expected to reach round three at the first attempt.

But to the disgust of the fans, so used to title-chasing and cup-hunting over the past five years, Arsenal did not even scrape a replay. Tranmere won 1–0 and we all sensed that things would never be the same again. We were right.

A few days later, on Saturday, 6 October 1973, I reported, as I'd been instructed on the Friday afternoon, with the first team, who faced a home game against Birmingham City.

I know that every player recalling his debut claims that he knew nothing about it until the last minute and that he was totally surprised. But that was honestly the case when Bertie Mee told me that I was down as substitute.

After all those weeks of hoping, when the moment came I was genuinely taken aback. Too much seemed to be happening in the club for it to be my turn, or so I believed.

I remember looking around the dressing room before the game, seeing Bob Wilson getting changed, Pat Rice and Bob McNab chatting with George Armstrong, big 'Raddy' quietly going about his business. But I also noticed that neither Alan Ball nor Charlie George were there. Their influence would be missed, though injuries were the reason for their absence, nothing more.

Just running out with the team and warming up in the pre-match kick-about was an experience like nothing I had known before.

I sensed, rather than saw, a sea of faces, and felt that they were all staring at me, wondering who I was, what I was like, whether I could change the team.

Then, quicker than it ever seemed when I used to watch games, the kick-in ended and I trotted back to the dug-out. That's that, I thought, and settled back in my tracksuit to absorb as much of the atmosphere as I could.

For all the Complan and iron, I was still slight, still seventeen and still raw. Arsenal were simply blooding me for the coming changes. But with only five minutes gone, Jeff Blockley twisted his knee and I knew in my bones that he would not be able to carry on.

Cruel as it sounds, I became really excited and could just about contain myself and keep watching the match. You know when a player has suffered an injury that neither sponge nor spray will heal. So by the time I was told to start warming up my stomach was coiled up like a spring.

Finally Jeff could not carry on. So I stepped out to show them all what I could do . . . and to my amazement, did just that! I played what is usually described as a 'blinder'. Ray Kennedy scored a first-half goal that proved enough to give us both points. But I could feel it inside me that I had done well.

After the match I came in contact with the press for the first time. Looking back I realize that they must have been struggling to find something at Arsenal to write about. Things were not exactly bubbling and my arrival on the scene gave them a headline.

But on the day I really thought I'd made it, arrived, broken through into the big-time. I stood in the hall and answered questions about where I came from, how long I'd been at the club, what I thought of the team, of Birmingham, of the weather . . . you name it, I was asked it. And, of course, at seventeen I could not believe this was happening to me.

One week later my world collapsed around my burning and embarrassed ears. Named in the team to meet North London rivals Spurs, at White Hart Lane, I could not wait to play in front of what was guaranteed to be a crowd of more than 40,000 partisan fans.

The result? Spurs 2, Arsenal 0, Brady nightmare.

Peter Simpson and Eddie Kelly played in the centre of the defence, Brendan Batson came on as substitute for 'Raddy', and me? Well I just kept praying for a divot large enough to swallow me. Nothing I tried came off, nothing I did went right. If ever a youngster experienced the absolute high and low of the game in one week, that youngster was Liam Brady.

From playing my way into the team after my display against Birmingham, I played my way out of it again at Spurs.

What's more I learned a hard and sore lesson about swaggering around, thinking you've made the grade. The senior players must have disliked me a bit for the way I behaved then, thinking, as I did, that things were going to be special from then on and that I was now one of them, an equal.

I can see the youngsters at Arsenal doing the very same thing and I have to laugh. It's too harsh to blame them. The whole game is geared to confidence and a little cockiness and self-belief. The trouble is that when you are that age you start to swan around and lord it over your mates of the day before. And when you fall, you come down with a mighty thump.

That's why I believe that the younger you get a lad into the League side for a taste of the big-time, the better equipped he becomes to handle his career when it takes off for real.

So back I went to the Reserves. I knew I had shown something of what I could do. And Bertie Mee must have seen enough to convince him that he had a player in the making. He also realized, however, that I needed a bit more time in the Football Combination.

Mee was very good to me at this stage of my career.

He kept a careful eye on my progress and hand-picked games for me in the League.

An Eddie Kelly goal beat Norwich City at Carrow Road in the third round of the FA Cup, sparking hopes of a good Wembley run. So when I made my third League appearance, also against Norwich at Highbury on 12 January 1974, the team was eleventh in the table and a bit more settled.

At last I lined up alongside Alan Ball whose two goals, and total domination of midfield, gave me a first-hand example of just how good a player he is.

'Bally' is a phenomenal character. He is a winner by nature and always takes defeat personally. Off the field he is big-hearted, a great enthusiast about young players and a man who can talk about the game for hours and hours without showing the slightest sign of flagging. On the field he is a born leader and he leads by example.

Ball will run until he drops and drives on those around him, demanding perfection and showing no mercy to those who fall below standards or those who make mistakes.

His game is built around the short pass, the prompt that dictates possession and the game's tempo. He has the ability to control the midfield because of his reading of situations and the speed at which his brain works.

Even when he does not have the ball – and usually he is yelling for it or tackling for it – Ball's influence can be overwhelming. He will issue non-stop instructions, pushing one man wide, another further forward, another deeper and so on.

This keeps the pressure on the opposition who can, if 'Bally' gets his own way, be browbeaten into centring their whole game around countering his!

To say that you learn a lot about football by playing alongside Alan Ball is an understatement. His very presence is an inspiration, especially when you are up against it during a game and looking for leadership.

Add to these qualities total, blunt honesty, consistently good finishing and a fearlessness that has often led him into trouble with officialdom because of his quick tongue and stinging criticisms, and you have a near-complete picture of Alan Ball.

Mee put me back in the Reserves for two weeks. The team

drew 1–1 at Old Trafford, then the next week Aston Villa came to Highbury for the fourth round of the Cup. Ray Kennedy earned a 1–1 draw, but Villa won the replay 2–0 and our season was as good as over.

But, for me, it meant a return to the first team, this time against Burnley at Highbury on 2 February. 'Bally' scored in a 1–1 draw and I felt that my feet were slowly settling into the League game.

My first away game for Arsenal was also the day I first met John Giles, the man who introduced me to international football and did so much to change the image of the Irish national team.

'Bally' put us ahead at half-time, but big Joe Jordan scored twice in a 3–1 Leeds triumph. Any disappointment I felt was instantly gone when I met Giles.

He was injured at the time and watched the game from the stand. Afterwards he approached me and talked to me as if I were a seasoned pro.

And there was I, looking, and feeling, dumbstruck. One of the players I had admired as a park player in Dublin, a man I had pretended to be in so many blood and thunder kick-abouts, was standing there, asking me about my game, my ambitions, my likes and dislikes.

I have always respected John. As a player he compared with the best in the history of the game. And as a manager he lifted West Bromwich Albion off their backsides and laid the foundations for Ron Atkinson to develop. But more than that, he went home to his native Dublin and revitalized the Republic of Ireland set-up to such an extent that we came to Wembley in September, 1976 and drew 1–1 with England in a game we should have won.

He was already manager of the Irish team when I met him, so you can imagine all the things going through my mind as we talked. I knew for a fact that I had played a reasonable game at Elland Road.

Things began to sour a bit when Spurs came to Highbury and beat us 1–0 in front of nearly 39,000 fans. A first-half goal by Chris McGrath, later to join Manchester United, made him the toast of one half of North London that night. But it seemed to plunge us backwards because the evening papers – we had them on Saturdays in those days – showed us in fifteenth place.

Yet destiny already had a number of things up its sleeve for me. I made further appearances against Birmingham and Ipswich, and came on as substitute against Manchester City. Then a gap before I came back as sub in a 3–1 defeat at Wolves on 15 April.

But it was in the last game of the season that so much happened to alter the course of my career.

I was named as substitute for the game against Queen's Park Rangers at Highbury on 30 April. We needed two points to finish top London team and a crowd of more than 40,000 turned up. Rangers were eighth and we were tenth, and that's the way it seemed likely to stay when Stan Bowles put them ahead in the first half.

It was not the goal, however, that sticks in my memory. It was the fact that Alan Ball broke a leg – an injury that brought me off the bench, into the battle and up into the box to score my first League goal.

The game ended 1–1, but my delight with scoring was spoiled by the thought of 'Bally' lying on the treatment table, knowing that his worst fears were being confirmed. He faced a long, lonely and painful summer. Yet he was determined to be fit fot the start of the next season.

If I had known what was going on behind my back at this time, however, I would have been so angry that nothing else would have mattered.

At the time I felt good because I had made nine full First Division appearances, faced some of the best players in Europe, added four more games to my tally as substitute and finally scored my first goal. That was more than enough to return to Dublin and discuss.

But John Giles had other plans for me. And I did not know about them.

Apparently he remembered me from that day at Leeds and decided he wanted to take me with the Irish international squad, preparing for a three-match tour of South America! They were scheduled to play Brazil, Chile and Uruguay and I might have won my first cap as a substitute. But when

John Giles approached Bertie Mee, he turned down his offer . . . without even consulting me.

I know that I was still a teenager, eighteen and pretty raw. But I believed that I had the right to be at least informed if not actually asked.

Mee told Giles that he believed I was too young to go on such a trip because I had experienced a hard season and needed more time before taking on such a responsibility.

Even if Mee had told me about the selection, then told me I was not going, I would have been disappointed but prepared to abide by my manager's decision.

As it was, they went away and did really well, beating Chile 2–1 and only losing 2–1 to Brazil. And there was I, delighted as the results reached Dublin, unaware that I could have been out there with them.

I never learned about John Giles's approach until I returned to Highbury for the start of the next season, 1974–75. I went to see Bertie Mee, as all players do at the start of a new campaign and talked about my progress and so on. Then it came out and I was furious. I had a real go at Mee there and then. I told him that I had a right to be consulted and that his actions were high-handed and totally unfair.

To the man's credit he said: 'Liam, I admit I was wrong and I apologize.' Well, what can anybody say to an answer like that? The subject was dropped and never mentioned again.

I was bubbling with anticipation as we packed for our pre-season European tour.

The changes were still going on behind the scenes. And to be honest, Charlie and 'Bally' were still unhappy with life at Highbury.

Ray Kennedy's weight problem did not help his game and he seemed to lose his edge as a front-runner. The partnership with 'Raddy' was over.

So when I heard that Ray had been transferred to Liverpool, where he became Bill Shankly's last signing, I was not so shocked.

It goes without saying that the move made Ray a tremendous player. The change of role from that of the target man, getting whacked in the back every five minutes, to that of midfield, from where the game opens up before you, revealed Ray to be a player of enormous talent.

Bob Wilson's retirement opened the way for Jimmy Rimmer to claim the first-team goalkeeping spot from Geoff Barnett.

Brian Kidd arrived from Manchester United to replace Ray Kennedy in mid-season and later that season, Jeff Blockley was transferred to Leicester City as Arsenal gradually changed faces, pushing the 'double' memory further and further back.

But for me, it became a crucial season midway through our first pre-season friendly in Holland. Alan Ball, who battled bravely, and successfully, to overcome the broken leg to such an extent that he was fit for the start of the new season, badly damaged it again and was carried off.

At that miserable moment, I realized that the way was clear for me to fight for a first-team place from the opening League game.

I knew that with so many changes in the air, it was up to players like me to prove that we were the new Arsenal. In the Reserves were Frank Stapleton and David O'Leary, making tremendous progress. The youngsters in the club were already earning rave reports which filtered up through the ranks to the top of the club.

A new era? A new style? New stars? Sorry as I felt for 'Bally', his injury gave me a chance to begin the season as a first-teamer. This unfortunate 'ill wind that blows nobody any good' situation occurs time and time again in football.

It is a mistake to allow yourself to feel any sense of guilt because you are pleased to make the most of another player's misfortune.

This is a risk we all take. And I know that the moment injury strikes me some player will step into my shirt very sharply and do his level best to stop me from getting it back.

The game is one in which there is no room for the meek or the mild. It is a competitive profession, geared to winners and cruel to losers.

4

Debut for Ireland

The day Ireland beat Russia 3–0 in Dublin in a European Championship qualifying tie was also the day I stepped out of Arsenal's protective arms and experienced a whole new world.

I made my international debut on that 30 October 1974, a memorable debut because of the result and the atmosphere that gripped Dublin for days afterwards.

John Giles was player-manager, so I knew that my first big occasion at international level would not be such a test. Giles is the type of character who guides other players through a game while playing his own game, almost effortlessly.

But long after our victory, and the celebrations and talk of the national team turning a very important corner in terms of prestige, I was aware of Arsenal's problems all the more, simply because I was away from the club for a short period and at last had something with which to make a comparison.

There we were, a mixed bunch of pros from varying levels of the game, clinically dismantling the soccer might of Russia in front of a fanatical crowd.

The place was absolutely electric, it made my blood pump fast and my scalp tingle. The dressing room was a babble of happy voices – jokers, boasters, justifiably proud Irishmen who were determined not to let the moment slip away from them.

How different it all seemed when compared with the cold and clammy hand of disenchantment tightening its grip on Arsenal. All of a sudden the bickering and bad results, the unhappy fans and long-faced directors, the nagging press, and even the worried doormen . . . all seemed miles away.

I knew that I was making good and steady progress as a First

Division player. And I suppose I was too young to realize that feeling happy with the way things were shaping for me was something I should have felt along with a concern about the team as a whole, not instead of!

Dublin – home, friends, family, success – all the things I wanted were there in those marvellous few days. Yet I thought of our squad at Highbury and of how strong it was. We should have been doing better. Something was terribly wrong.

So much about football is also about confidence – in yourself, your team-mates, your manager and your supporters. The Irish team had all those things that October night. Arsenal seemed to have none of them.

From Paddy Roche in goal to Steve Heighway on the wing we were a unit. Don Givens scored a fine hat-trick, everyone did his bit and all the factors that go towards making football a great life were there for me to see and understand.

On the journey back to England I re-ran a kind of mental tape and thought back to the beginning of the season and to the moment when I realized that 'Bally's' injury on tour meant an almost certain place for me in the team.

Despite the comings and goings, we still had a very good squad. The fans must have expected more than they got. But they could not have known of the disputes and personality clashes which were evident from the start of the season and got worse as the months went by.

Although they became friends and team-mates later, at Southampton, it was obvious to all of us that Alan Ball and Charlie George did not get on. Charlie believed that he was the best player at the club. And, in fairness, when he put his mind and body to it, he was. But those occasions were too few and far between, and Charlie was simply disillusioned with Arsenal overall.

I have no doubt that most young lads today have heard the expression 'so-and-so's playing to get away from the club'. Well that is precisely what people thought Charlie was doing.

On the opening day of the season we played Leicester City at Filbert Street. I lined up wearing the number 11 shirt – my first season as a first-teamer from the 'off' – and a Brian Kidd goal in the second half was enough to give us two points.

We were pleased and optimistic. So were the fans because more than 31,000 turned up on the Tuesday night at Highbury to see us play Ipswich. But we lost 1–0, played badly and immediately the dressing-room rucking began all over again. It was plain to see that the players were not happy, and one bad result brought this out.

'Kiddo' enjoyed his first home goals on Saturday, 24 August scoring twice in a 4–0 win at Highbury over Manchester City. But any hopes we had that this would spark a take-off of the changing Arsenal side were smashed the following Wednesday as we slumped to a 2–1 defeat at Everton. Kidd scored again, but his success was an isolated one. The team was spluttering and heading for a run of ten First Division games without a win.

We nosedived to the bottom of the table, and for the first time, the private, well-concealed mumblings grew into audible complaints.

The press have never shown any great love for Arsenal. Even during their most successful seasons there seemed to exist some strange resentment, almost a jealousy, about everything the club won.

So, as you may imagine, they took delight in giving us good pannings, week after week, and this, naturally, did wonders for flagging morale!

Oddly enough, although I was a regular member of the team and played in all of those winless games, I still seemed a little bit of an outsider because I was not involved in any of the real rows. I suppose I was too new on the scene.

But it was uncomfortable to be in the middle of rows. I remember trying to avoid looking at any one person for too long in case it was misinterpreted as a form of involvement or taking sides.

Sometimes there would be a prolonged silence after coming off the pitch. Then one player would comment on a mistake or misunderstanding from the game and another would immediately react defensively.

Such flashes of sensitivity were really only the symptoms. The disease was the overall discontent, the smouldering anger of players with reputations who felt they were getting nowhere

Two pictures that tell more than a thousand words – (*above*) my first break in the big time. That's me, far right of the back row, still waiting for my kit. (*Below*) a memorable match against World Champions Argentina. We drew 0–0 with the brilliant South Americans in my native Dublin

I joined Arsenal a few months after they clinched the 1971 League and FA Cup 'double' by beating Liverpool 2–1 at Wembley. Here (*above*) Frank McLintock shows the trophy to the fans. Little did I know that the next time Arsenal won the Cup, I would play a part! (*below*)

The most emotional and satisfying moment of my career – winning the 1979
FA Cup. I was too happy to be worried by some people's grouses about
swopping shirts!

Annoying though it was, we were all confident that Gordon McQueen's 86th minute goal in the 1979 Cup Final wouldn't affect the result

After Sammy McIlroy stunned us with the equalizer, my only thought was to carry the ball deep into United's half and away from our goal

and playing in a team which was simply not as well-balanced as it should have been.

It was in October that Bertie Mee shocked football by signing Terry Mancini from QPR for a reported £20,000. Terry, a natural comedian and tremendous spirit-raiser in the dressing room, replaced Blockley at centre-half and quickly established himself as a character and a crowd favourite.

That bald head would rise above the most expensive strikers in the game and nod the ball to safety while everyone seemed to hold their breath, waiting for Terry to be found out.

A great footballer he was not. But he did the job he was bought to do and made such a warming impact that he was eventually appointed club captain.

Terry, with an Italian name, a Cockney accent and Irish parentage, won his fifth Ireland cap on the night I made my debut. We discussed a lot of things, and he was helpful to me, providing a calm, experienced approach to football problems and also a good-humoured approach to almost everything.

I remember reading, time and again, that Terry was the great dressing-room wag, keeping the players doubled up with laughter. He had the personality to do just that. But unfortunately, most of the players did not find him funny at that time. They had too much on their minds – and it left no room for being light-hearted.

As quickly as it had begun, though, our dreadful run ended, and ended in magnificent style.

Our supporters stayed remarkably loyal through the run which, for Arsenal, was nothing short of disastrous, and more than 36,000 were there to see us beat West Ham 3–0 on 26 October.

The goals came from John Radford, Brian Kidd and myself, and the result was just the boost all of us needed. Wolves held us to a 0–0 draw at Highbury the next week, but it was a more confident Arsenal that set out for the daunting prospect of facing Liverpool at Anfield.

The lads were naturally in much better spirits than for some time. And I was especially happy as the win against West Ham came at the end of the week in which I'd made my international debut.

49

It never ceases to amaze me how football fortunes can rise and fall so quickly. I imagine that, if we had played at Liverpool three weeks earlier, they would have found us tense, anxious and virtually devoid of confidence. But three points from two games and the clouds were lifted.

Alan Ball was at his majestic best, running the game from midfield and scoring two goals in our 3–1 win into the bargain. I had the pleasure of scoring our other goal in a victory that at any time is worth shouting about, but in our particular case merited genuine celebration.

We were as pleased for the fans as we were for ourselves. I remember the trip home to London during which a number of players confirmed how relieved they were to ease the pressure – in the dressing-rooms and in hundreds of North London pubs and clubs.

Something else pleased me greatly, and that was the growing confidence with which I was playing and the knowledge that Bertie Mee had enough faith in me to keep me in the team when Alan Ball returned to full fitness.

So from being in only because he was unavailable, I knew that I had carved a bit of a niche for myself, in my own right. I was contributing to the team at a time when things were a bit unsettled. Mee saw this as a sign of even better things to come.

The awful pity is that he did not see that it was too early to break up his 'double' side. I have no doubt that he would agree with me now. And it is easy for me to sit down and pen such an opinion in hindsight. But in fairness, a lot of those players left from the 'double' side were saying the same thing even as Bertie was planning to build a whole new Arsenal.

He was selling top-class players like Ray Kennedy, Frank McLintock and George Graham. But, with all due respect, the players who came in as replacements were not in the same class.

But we plugged away, hoping for something to come out of our FA Cup campaign. Leicester dumped us out of the League Cup as early as the second round. I scored my first Cup goal for the club, but we lost a replay 2–1 after a 1–1 draw.

For a while, everything went well, especially for me. I

believed I was holding my place on merit, and was also making sure that I remembered how much I still had to learn. I did things simply and watched the senior players closely.

We followed up our shock win at Anfield by beating Derby 3–1 at home, 'Bally' again scoring twice. Coventry brought us down to earth – and one place back down the table to nineteenth – with a 3–0 win at Highfield Road, but we immediately picked up the tempo again, beating Middlesbrough 2–0 at home. I scored the first, 'Bally' hit a penalty and we could all feel ourselves getting a firmer footing on the season.

It was then that Mee spent £150,000 to bring Alex Cropley down from Hibernian. I knew enough about him to realize that the one place in the side tailor-made for his game was mine, as he was a natural left-sided midfield player.

Despite my age I knew deep down that I was playing well. But I took notice of the newspaper stories which suggested that I would be axed to make room for Alex, and my spirits sank.

I went straight to see Mee and Campbell and told them both that I sincerely hoped it was not going to be me who was dropped. They both assured me that I was staying in the team and I left the office relieved but a little puzzled. Common sense told me that it was unlikely that a club would pay so much money for a player, then stick him in the Reserves.

We were due to play at Carlisle on 7 December, but when I read the team sheet my name was not on it. Mee and Campbell had lied to me. Looking back I probably took them by surprise when I marched into the office and made my feelings known. But I do know that my relationship with them was never the same again.

I developed a nagging pelvic strain while playing in the Reserves and was told to take a two-month rest. It proved to be my longest spell out of the Arsenal team through injury. I was fortunate in that playing for the Reserves I was able to get it put right. Had I been in the first team I might have opted to keep on playing rather than lose my place, and possibly aggravated the injury.

On 4 January 1975 Arsenal drew 1–1 at home to York in the FA Cup third round. We were a struggling nineteenth in Division One at the time, but they were in the bottom half of the

Second Division and our fans let us know how disgusted they were with the result.

I missed the replay of that tie on 7 January. Brian Kidd put Arsenal ahead, but Barry Lyons equalized and it required two more from the prolific Kidd in extra time to see the team safely into the fourth round. I was still in with a chance of making my full FA Cup debut.

I returned to the team on 1 February. Two more goals from 'Bally' sank Liverpool 2–0 at Highbury to lift us to fifteenth in the table. But Charlie George had already submitted one of a number of transfer requests and this time it was granted. We knew this meant another top-class player on the way out.

Personally I was very excited about the FA Cup and wrapped up in my hopes that we could go all the way.

The lads – again without me – had held Coventry 1–1 at Highfield Road on 24 January in the fourth round, and won the replay 3–0 at Highbury three days later. I stepped into FA Cup action as substitute for John Radford.

On 15 February, two days after my nineteenth birthday, we made a mess of our fifth round tie at home to Leicester, draw- ing 0–0. I was left out of the replay, John Matthews replacing me, but came on as sub as the team battled to a 1–1 draw after extra time.

We finally edged into the quarter-finals with a second replay winner from 'Raddy', again after extra time and I repeated my job as active sub for Matthews.

But any reasons for celebration were dampened by incidents which rocked the club on 22 February, two days before that second replay.

We played Derby County at The Baseball Ground, lost 2–1, slipped back to eighteenth in the table . . . and 'Bally' and Bob McNab were both sent off.

It was only the second time since the Second World War that two players from the same team were sent off in one game. And Arsenal were not very happy about it.

After a lot of deliberations the club announced that it was not going to support the players' appeal – a decision which enraged Bally to the point where he told us: 'Arsenal and I can never be the same again.' Arsenal's decision angered the whole team because we had a cup quarter-final coming up, and needed both players – in those days a suspension was delayed until an appeal was heard.

And we did nothing to heal the growing breach between team and fans when we tumbled out of the Cup at home to West Ham United. Bally and Bob appealed without the club's support, and won the opportunity to play in the tie. But by then the damage was done and the squad upset once more.

On 1 March we lost 2–0 at home to Everton, then one week later, in front of more than 56,000 people, fell at the hands of a young lad named Alan Taylor, destined to score two goals in the quarter-final, semi-final and Final.

It was a terrible blow because our season – achieving First Division survival apart – was a dead duck.

Now, like some tidal wave cracking a wall, the frustrations, worries and anger of the players swept through the corridors.

Players clashed amongst themselves. Some were unhappy with what they considered to be Mee's lack of interest in the team. Others were not satisfied with Bobby Campbell's coaching. And those sitting on the fence were just unhappy because the whole place was depressing.

Bertie Mee had experienced the absolute heights of success with the club. With Howe coaching and working with the players at the training level, Mee concentrated on his greatest managerial strength – man-management.

But it seemed to lose impact as things went wrong. After Howe's move to West Bromwich, it was as if Mee lost a measure of effectiveness.

We saw less and less of him. And because we were worried about the team's form and what we considered to be a non-too-rosy future, our fears that Mee was becoming increasingly distant and uninvolved were heightened.

Bobby Campbell tried very hard to stimulate the players. But it was too late. His coaching methods simply did not create any new spark. He tried, without success, to get the best out of the squad. But we began to consider a lot of the work predictable and therefore unlikely to improve the way we were playing.

It is all too easy to lay the blame at Campbell's door. There was more to it than that. But he was the man we saw, day in, day out. And he must have become infected by the atmosphere.

It must have been reflected in the way the team played. One game, a 1–0 home win over Sheffield United thanks to yet another Kidd goal, brought a furious outburst from United manager Ken Furphy who said: 'I never thought I would live to see the day when Arsenal players fought amongst themselves, pulled shirts, wasted time and so freely indulged in foul tactics.'

In fairness this dramatic statement was closer to hysteria than it was the truth, but nonetheless the team was not pretty to watch. I was not playing that day, and to be honest I was a bit confused by the way events were taking shape.

Even at nineteen I could sense a civil war on the horizon. It was less than a season away, and almost split the club in half.

My most vivid memory of this time was the repeated comparisons that my appearances for Ireland allowed me to make. I looked forward to joining the squad, not just because of what it meant to represent my country, but also because it was nice, especially at nineteen, to be surrounded by happier pros, men without such intensity on their faces and such knitted eyebrows.

On 20 November we flew out to play Turkey in Izmir and drew 1–1. Once again the camp was a settled and happy one. Giles, still playing as well as managing, was steadily creating an international squad with a club-like atmosphere.

And with three points from our first two European Championship qualifying games, we knew that a win over Switzerland in Dublin in the next game would establish us group favourites . . . and guarantee us the freedom of Dublin.

The Turks gave a typical passionate performance in front of a 67,000 crowd, but Don Givens scored our point-winner and we even scored their goal for them, a tragic own goal by Mick Martin after half-time. The press 'credited' the goal to Terry Conroy, but I feel I must take him off the hook after all this time!

The season at Arsenal finished like a damp firework. We were a safe fifteenth in the table, but only Brian Kidd, Jimmy Rimmer, and Alan Ball among the seniors had true reason to be happy with their overall form.

I was pleased from a personal point of view because I made thirty League appearances, scoring three goals, at a time when things were rocky and the team constantly being reshuffled.

Deep down I suppose I knew that the bickering and divisions within the squad could not continue without something giving. The new season would have to be decisive, one way or the other.

But as I left behind the domestic problems for the excitement of international progress with Ireland, I could not have known just how correct my fears would prove to be concerning the forthcoming 1975–76 season.

Another young Dubliner was also on the verge of a genuine breakthrough. Frank Stapleton, whose single appearance in season 1974–75 on 29 March against Stoke at Highbury ended in defeat, nevertheless showed through consistent scoring for the Reserves that his time as a First Division player was drawing close.

Meanwhile this Dubliner took his place in the Ireland team for a game that was to bring my native city alight once again and set us up as Group Six favourites, against all previous expectations.

A crowd of 50,000 jammed Lansdowne Road for our match against the Swiss, and we did not disappoint them.

First-half goals by Mick Martin and Ray Treacy knocked the yodels out of the Swiss and, with the crowd in full voice, the game seemed completely in our control.

The third goal we wanted to wrap it up safely would not come. Then Muller snatched one back and we endured some groggy moments before emerging with the five points from six that we so badly wanted.

As you can imagine, the atmosphere was unbelievable. Nobody outside Ireland gave us a cat in hell's chance when we were paired with the Russians. All we needed was a draw in Kiev on 18 May and the Group Six table would have been virtually beyond everyone but us.

Sadly, as is often the case, things never seem to go as we plan them when we go away from home.

John Giles made one change, bringing in Steve Heighway

for Ray Treacy, and we gave a tremendous account of ourselves in front of 100,000 roaring Russians. This time it was our turn to change ends the wrong side of a two-goal deficit, but when Eoin Hand halved the deficit we threw everything we could at them, but could not force the draw.

Far from disheartened by such a display behind the Iron Curtain, we planned for the return with the Swiss in Zurich where we had high hopes of catching them at a low football ebb. But our disappointing performance on 21 May cost us qualification. We lost 1–0 to a second-half goal by Elsener, undoing all the good work achieved in Dublin.

From my point of view, the whole experience was one of tremendous high points and sickening disappointment. But it was also a great time for a boy of nineteen to enjoy. John Giles allowed me a certain amount of freedom on the pitch, always ready to give help and advice if I required it.

In some ways, I learned as much about the game at top level from Giles in those few internationals, as I did from a whole season with Arsenal.

Giles managed the Ireland team using all the knowledge he acquired from a brilliant career with Manchester United, Leeds United and West Bromwich Albion. He found out how hard the game can be when Manchester United transferred him to Leeds after he had helped them to beat Leicester City 3–1 in the 1963 FA Cup Final.

A right-winger in those days, he wanted to make an impression at Old Trafford. But he overcame the disappointment of being discarded and with the help of Don Revie, switched to midfield and became one of the great players of the era.

Giles saw all sides of the game during his playing career, the way Revie got the best out of Billy Bremner and Jack Charlton, the way he lifted experienced professionals after repeated disappointments and ultimately led them to remarkable triumphs.

At Albion he achieved what many people believed to be impossible at that level, succeeding as a player-manager and driving the club to promotion to the First Division.

He applied the same common-sense approach with the international team. Like Revie, Giles believes in strong discipline, a close-knit squad, loyalty among players and basic hard work. He does not mince words, speaks his mind to your face and always leaves his door ajar if a player wants to discuss a problem. He commands respect and shows no favouritism.

And at that time, he offered all the strengths missing from Highbury.

But then an awful lot has to do with an atmosphere. And, as I pointed out, the Arsenal atmosphere was negative while Ireland's was positive.

No matter how gifted a young lad may be, he requires the correct advice – which I got – and the correct instruction – which Arsenal also gave me. But he needs a strong, positive, united atmosphere within his team for the boy to gain real confidence and express himself. This we did not have. And it was destined to get worse before getting infinitely better.

5

A Tale of Two Associations

Ireland produces some of the best footballers in the world. Yet the country is still waiting to be recognized as an international force comparable with the likes of Italy, England, West Germany and Holland.

I believe that if it were possible to select the eleven best Irish players of the moment – be that moment now or ten years time – and field a team called 'Ireland', without the troublesome prefix of 'Northern' or 'Republic of', that team would make the rest of the world sit up and watch.

Unfortunately, because of political bitterness and historical differences, this ideal situation is still some way short of happening.

I deliberately avoid using the words 'cannot happen' because I believe it can.

You cannot blame the rest of the world for thinking 'it could only happen in that country' when they see sports page headlines which, removing the political trimmings, amount to: IRELAND 0, IRELAND 0!

But that is the sad reality of international football in my divided homeland. However, there is no reason why it has to continue to be divided where football is concerned.

I blame selfishness and, to some extent, ignorance on the part of both sets of governing bodies for the fact that Ireland has to produce two international teams, to face the best the world has to offer, from an island with a population less than one third that of London.

The tragedy of it all is that every professional footballer from

58

Ireland that I have spoken with wants the same thing – a united Ireland team.

Some people may believe that a mixture of apathy and bigotry on the part of the players is to blame for the current situation.

Nothing could be further from the truth. And if you analyse the position rationally, it becomes obvious.

We are in football to make a living, to play the game we love more than anything else, to be successful, and to reach and compete against the highest levels of the profession.

So it stands to reason that Irishmen want one team as their international platform, one team capable of taking on the likes of Holland and Italy, England and West Germany, and beating them.

Day dreaming? I would not be so sure. If every Irish player, from the North and the South, became unavailable for Football League duty, a large percentage of England's top clubs would find it difficult to replace them.

And when you consider the relative success the two representative sides do achieve, in spite of the fact that the overall best players are shared between two squads, it makes you wonder just what we might achieve if united.

One fact cannot be escaped. Ireland has won the Home International Championship outright only once – in 1914. And that was before the political troubles that split the nation . . . and the football team.

Northern Ireland have managed to share the title with the others on a handful of occasions since. All four home countries finished on three points in 1956; England and Northern Ireland shared the title on four points in 1958 and 1959; England, Scotland and Northern Ireland shared it on four points in 1964. But those isolated occasions apart, Ulster's realistic hopes of taking that British title are remote.

How do you think those Ulstermen feel when they know that, if united with the players from the other side of some wooden pole or sentry box – usually imaginary – they could achieve so much more?

I don't have to imagine how they feel. I know. I have shared many a conversation on this subject with my Arsenal team-mates. And I share their frustration.

The history of Irish football is studded with top-class players. It is a fact that they usually come to England to make their names because England has one of the world's strongest and most competitive Leagues.

But this, in turn, leads people to believe that the country is a football minnow. This is simply not true.

What is true is that I am very proud to share the international heritage of players such as George Best, surely the greatest player in the world during his peak with Manchester United.

George and I are Irishmen. Yet we never had the opportunity of playing in the same international team. To my bitter disappointment I never even played against him at that level. And I believe that is utterly daft.

Looking back I can instantly recall players who were dazzling the world with their skills even when I was at school in Dublin.

Billy Bingham of Sunderland, Luton, Everton and later Port Vale, won fifty-six caps for Northern Ireland and shone for them in the 1958 World Cup in Sweden when they reached the Finals, and beat Czechoslovakia 1–0 before drawing 2–2 with eventual semi-finalists West Germany.

Also part of that great Irish team was Danny Blanchflower whose contribution to Tottenham Hotspur's 1961 League and FA Cup 'double' is legendary. Danny played for Barnsley, Aston Villa and Spurs and won fifty-six Irish caps, ultimately emulating Bingham's feat of becoming national manager.

Johnny Carey, the great Manchester United defender, won seven caps for Northern Ireland . . . and twenty-nine for the Republic between 1938 and 1953. But at that time it was possible to cross the border and play for both sides!

Another famous player to achieve this unusual distinction was Con Martin, father of current Eire international Mick Martin.

Con, a gifted player who played international football in goal and on the field, made six appearances for the North and thirty for the South between 1946 and 1956.

Martin was a class player who began his career with

60

Glentoran before playing League football for Aston Villa and Leeds United.

Jimmy McIlroy won fifty-five Northern Ireland caps with Burnley and Stoke; John Crossan won twenty-three while playing for Sparta Rotterdam, Sunderland, Manchester City and Middlesbrough; the great Peter Doherty's career with Blackpool, Manchester City, Derby County, Huddersfield and Doncaster Rovers brought him sixteen caps.

It becomes all too easy to roll their names off your tongue as would a fan flicking through his scrap-book – Derek Dougan, Alex Elder, Martin Harvey, Sammy McIlroy, Willie Irvine, Allan Hunter, Peter McParland, Martin O'Neill, Elisha Scott. . . .

A mixture of talents from a jumble of eras. I know that. But it is unusual for a man to think in alphabetical order, and players come to mind for a whole range of reasons.

And what, you might ask, about my team-mates at Arsenal? Well I've reserved a special place for them.

Look again at that list of marvellous players and the first thing that strikes you is that they all come under the category of being eligible only for Northern Ireland.

The rest of us stand on the other side of that man-made border wondering what the hell politics has to do with football. When you see the Irish rugby team doing so well year after year, with men from all Ireland's corners, you cannot help but feel puzzled and angry at the stupidity of it all.

As I said, with the exception of Carey and Martin, whose careers happened to span an era of loop-holes, those great names were – and still are in current cases – hemmed in by a force stronger than their united wish for a national team to sweep the board.

The Republic has produced its equal share of top players – Shay Brennan, John Giles, Noel Cantwell, Gerry Daly, Steve Heighway, Pat Dunne, Mick McGrath, Don Givens, Alan Kelly, Charlie Hurley. . . . Perming a suitable eleven from any given era would have surely produced a team stronger than any the two Associations often struggled to produce in the past.

Today is no different and good examples of what I mean immediately come to mind.

The day the European Championship groups were named, six Irishmen at Highbury sat down and faced up to a sickening and depressing reality.

Pat Jennings, David O'Leary, Frank Stapleton, Sammy Nelson, Pat Rice and myself all agreed that we were going to do our best to ensure that exactly half that gathering's international hopes failed.

We analysed the grouping of England, Denmark and Bulgaria with Northern Ireland and the Irish Republic. Not the least of the talking points was the inevitable first meeting between the two Irelands.

There we were, born on the same island yet destined to come face to face in combat and, as it turned out, wreck each other's chances of reaching the Italy-based Finals.

When you look closely at the results both teams achieved in the early qualifying games, the situation becomes all the sadder.

Eire drew 3–3 in Denmark on 24 May, 1978. But that dreaded day arrived in September when we were at home to Northern Ireland in Dublin.

I remember vividly how stupid and senseless the whole thing seemed. The public were apprehensive, probably anticipating all sorts of problems stemming from the political undertones. But it was played in a good spirit, leading a lot of spectators to label the game an anti-climax. I often wonder if they would have preferred a physical, nasty affair.

There was so much talk before the match, so many speculative headlines, that you cannot blame the punters for anticipating something out of the ordinary. In the end they got a 0–0 draw which was to prove a bad result for both teams.

I remember the 46,000 crowd's unusual atmosphere. As if there was something bizarre and unreal about the whole game.

There I was, in the same team as Frank Stapleton, facing Pat Jennings, Sammy Nelson and Pat Rice. And it seemed so ironic that both teams use green and white as their first choice colours.

After that, they beat Denmark 2–1 at Windsor Park in the October while we were drawing 1–1 with England, who were already understandable favourites to qualify. But in November, Northern Ireland shook Europe by winning 2–0 in Sofia. When we went there we lost 1–0 in a game we could and should have at least drawn.

The fact was that although we later beat Denmark 2–0 in Dublin in May 1979 and followed up this by hammering the Bulgarians 3–0 again in Dublin, it was all too late. England romped home 5–1 in Belfast, and the good results achieved by the two Irelands came to nothing.

Did the ruling bodies either side of the border sit up and take action after this foolishness? No they did not.

And as the 1982 World Cup groupings were announced, we considered the prospects of what by then was the Arsenal seven, John Devine giving the Republic a 4–3 advantage at Highbury.

Scotland and Portugal are among Northern Ireland's hurdles. We face Holland, France, Belgium and Cyprus. But why are we not united and taking on the best of one group?

The reasons are not difficult to unearth. Two ruling bodies means two lots of jobs and two separate powers. The problem is getting these Associations – the FA of Ireland and the Irish FA – to merge for the good of the country.

But it seems to me that these men are less willing to risk losing their places in the 'team' than the players.

It is a fact that many Irish players are prepared to accept the risk of losing their international places in order to secure a united team.

How many of the non-playing administrators can honestly make the same claim? Not many judging by the lack of activity in the respective Associations.

I believe that if they held a referendum among the Irish football fans, the border would be torn down, one set of green shirts thrown away and a national team would emerge, willing to alternate its games between Dublin and Belfast.

I am not saying that problems do not exist. Of course they do. Lots of them. But it is too easy to get half-way through a list of problems, then stop and declare the situation hopeless.

We are talking football now, not politics. And my personal experiences are that it makes no damn difference whether a player is a Republican or a Unionist. He is a professional first and foremost. He is also an Irishman with an understandable desire to parade his skills at the very highest level.

Irish players do want a united national team. I believe it is the people in official positions who are preventing such a team being formed.

Until we take a leaf out of the Irish Rugby Union's book, we will have to carry on playing as two nations, and that is a sad state of affairs.

6

Trouble on the Horizon

Refreshed by the summer break, and Ireland's European Championship campaign, I returned to Highbury full of hope for a season in which most of the young players at Arsenal were expected to produce the new-look team Bertie Mee and Bobby Campbell had promised.

By the time the season was over, the club was at its lowest ebb for decades, Mee and Campbell were gone, the fans were stunned by the battle their once-mighty team had to put up to stay in the First Division, and I had made the transition from boy to man.

It was a terrible time to be at Highbury. Senior players were soured by events, the backbone of the team wanted to go, the directors were unhappy with the players, the fans were unhappy with the board and the players, and all around me I saw one of the game's institutions being reduced to the level of a troubled giant.

I should have spotted the first signs of real trouble when Bally and I were selected to play for a Don Revie XI at Anfield in Bill Shankly's testimonial match, shortly before my return to Dublin for the internationals at the end of the previous season.

To my surprise, Bally revealed that he was tired and weary of the prospect of going through the grind of being the father-figure to a team of youngsters all over again.

That is not to say that he had lost interest in youngsters. Far from it. But the truth behind the man's disillusionment lay in the long, dark road he envisaged Arsenal tramping before they saw any success again.

His warning before that game was no idle threat. Because while I was playing for Ireland, Bally was composing a letter that, when finished, represented a transfer request.

Suddenly, from being Highbury's blue-eyed boy, he was out in the cold, dropped for the opening games of the 1975–76 season.

Eddie Kelly became team captain, and that was when Terry Mancini was officially appointed club captain. It looked as if the club had dispensed with Ball's services and were waiting for the right offer.

Eddie was very proud of his appointment and I remember him saying how he was going to make a good job of it and really get his game together again after a mediocre spell.

So, with the fans anxious to see the Arsenal young bloods fulfil the faith Mee had put in them, we took three points from two away games, 0–0 at Burnley and 3–1 at Sheffield United where I scored our first League goal of the campaign.

But once Stoke had beaten us 1–0 at home in the season's third game, all the old problems flooded back; and with them came the doubts and worries about the team just not being properly balanced, and the sad sight of seniors like Pat Rice, George Armstrong and Eddie Kelly fretting over the side's inconsistency.

Ball was brought back for the fourth game, scored a penalty in a 2–1 home win over Norwich and the fans relaxed slightly. But down in the dressing-room, no such respite. Eddie was worried about Bally's return simply because although still the new skipper, Eddie fell under Bally's shadow on the pitch.

I don't think Mee and Campbell ever realized how much this upset Eddie. He felt in a farcical situation as captain of a team which, instinctively, looked to Ball for captaincy when he was on the field. The man is a natural and, when he is around, nobody else can be skipper. But this was a situation Eddie could not accept.

This was just one factor destined to upset the atmosphere and, from beginning the season as Arsenal's proud new captain, Eddie ended it by leaving the club and joining Queen's Park Rangers.

But even before that season began, two further links with the great 'double' side were broken, and once again it meant the loss of two class players destined to be replaced by raw youngsters out of the Football Combination side.

On 2 July 1975 Charlie George finally got his wish. He was transferred to Derby County for a reported £90,000, and eight days later Bob McNab was given a free transfer and elected to join Wolves.

Mee tried to establish his authority with the new bunch of players by announcing that he was going to fine players who were booked for dissent.

But at the same time, the club's chief scout, Gordon Clark, launched a bitter attack on the youngsters, saying: 'Some of them need a kick up the backside. I am anxious for them to make the grade, but they will have to pull their fingers out.'

The needle was spreading throughout the club.

Everton knocked us out of the League Cup in the second round, winning a replay at Highbury 1–0 after a 2–2 draw at Goodison Park. And by November we were four places off the bottom of the table, attendances were well down, and nothing Mee and Campbell tried seemed to work quickly enough to get the team going.

Ironically, by the time the courage they showed in giving youngsters such as myself, David O'Leary, Frank Stapleton and Ritchie Powling our chance in the First Division was repaid through the team's success, Mee and Campbell were long gone. This is a good example to every lad coming into the game of how tough it can be on managers and coaches to blood youngsters when fans and directors want success instantly.

I have no doubt that Arsenal's Cup Finals and European runs were the result of young players being introduced to the side early enough to give them experience, confidence and the professional knowledge to put their ability to its fullest use.

But in the professional game success is the monster which needs to be fed game by game. It is no good promising season ticket holders of today a winning team in two years' time. They are likely to cancel their cheques and promise to issue them again in two years' time!

My own game, and my whole character, benefited during a season that for the senior players was undoubtedly a nightmare. People like me, Dave O'Leary, Frank Stapleton ... we were young and therefore forgiven mistakes for that reason. We, they said, would come good. But the older players were expected to perform.

When Bally asked to come off the transfer list that same November, it did some good for morale. But nowhere near enough. Confidence drained – visibly in certain cases. Why? Because at this level football is work, it is a living, it is the way the players pay for their mortgages, children's education, car bills and everyday living.

Just like any other job, it determines the standard of living of those men employed by clubs.

In Arsenal's case the senior players had grown up with success. They were used to regular win bonuses, regular crowd bonuses, end of season bonuses for honours won. Understandably the money they earned gave them a certain life style, a standard of living which demanded that their incomes should be maintained at a high level.

So when the team began to break up, when the youngsters came in and struggled to find their feet, when League Cup and FA Cup runs became shorter each season, the bonuses dried up. Men had to face the reality of dropping their living standards. Not at first. But the lengthy period of struggles we experienced during this time meant that the spell was broken, the cloud-nine days of healthy bank accounts were disappearing.

Human nature tells us that this must lead to anxiety, and perhaps some pressure from wives, equally worried by the unexpected drop in cash levels.

I am sure that the majority of fans rarely think of the game in this light. But as well as being a wonderful career and the best game in the world, it is also a job.

Watching the bitterness and sourness in the dressing-room, I quickly grew up. I learned to watch out for myself, especially after standing up during one of the many team meetings we had that season to say my piece, only to discover that certain players were quick to argue and take me to task for my opinions.

In this respect football clubs are the same as factories and offices. The employees belong to various unions. They hold meetings to thrash out problems, they make decisions that very often nobody takes any notice of anyhow, but everyone feels better for having made his and her point.

We were the very same, gathering for discussions over Mee, Campbell, the directors, the team's shortcomings, the system we were playing, general conditions and grumbles.

As you might expect, some of these meetings became heated and this often only made the atmosphere worse.

Having already gone through one unhappy season, I knew what Frank Stapleton and David O'Leary were going through as they made their first real breakthrough in the First Division. Certainly we tended to bond together. Not because we all come from Dublin, which a lot of people seem to expect, but because we were all young and learning our job.

In fact this extraordinary attitude has often puzzled me. The fact that we all come from Ireland should not have determined whether or not we became close friends and socialized outside the job. Naturally we were pals. But not to the 'Arsenal's Irish clan' degree which the press and public liked to believe.

Being realistic, if things had come to a crunch and fists were raised, I would have automatically sided with the other Irish players. But that is a natural reaction.

For away games, my room-mate was usually Ritchie Powling. We got on very well. But then all the young players got on. We were in the same situation – wanting to do well, wanting to help the team improve yet feeling somewhat responsible for the pressure under which the senior players were existing.

Wolves gave us a real FA Cup thumping at Molineux where we crashed out of the third round by 3–0. Once again our season was dead – just a dreary, worrying relegation battle.

This brought out the fighter in me. I was determined to come through and seemed to establish a consistency in an inconsistent team. Had I allowed the general depression to get to me too much, I doubt if my career would ever have developed.

Once again I had Ireland's international progress to cheer me up. We played Turkey in Dublin around this time and hammered them 4–0. Don Givens went one better than his personal display against Russia, scoring all four goals – a marvellous feat at any soccer level, let alone an international.

We had a bit of crowd trouble that led to a fine on the FA of Ireland by UEFA. The fans were wrong to misbehave, but they believed they were backing the team. This was something you could rarely say about the people who sat up in the seats at Highbury.

The fans who stand on the terraces are usually the majority of the people who travel with you to away games at the end of the earth and in the foulest weather. They back you as much as possible. But I have been astonished to look up at the stands while we were winning a game and seen the anger and fury on some blurred faces.

I suppose I could hear it rather than see it from that range, but I never understood why they were so critical. So, as you can imagine, those people were united in their criticism, usually very loud criticism, of the team during this troubled period. I genuinely felt sorry for the likes of John Radford, 'Geordie' Armstrong, Eddie Kelly and Pat Rice. They took some shocking stick.

One thing the fans could never say was that we were quitters. For all the squabbles and fears the team was made up of good pros and enthusiastic youngsters. We were proud to be playing for Arsenal. It fired the young players and kept the seniors going because, above all else, they were puzzled why so big a club should be sinking so low and did not want the world to believe that they had not shown enough interest and care.

The fact that we, as a team, began to suspect that the board and management did not care was to lead to the final confrontation.

Although you could hardly describe my scoring rate as prolific, I did contribute a few vital goals, something which gave me tremendous personal satisfaction. I wanted to be seen to be doing my bit to keep us afloat, especially as Bobby Campbell, the man who gave me my chance in the first place, gradually turned against me.

On 31 January 1976 I scored the goal which gave us a 1–0 home win over Sheffield United. We were eighteenth in the table again but it kept us with our heads above water.

Then another single goal proved enough to beat Birmingham, again at Highbury, on 21 February, but we were still dangerously close to going down. Wolves, Burnley and Birmingham were making a fight of it, and we knew that we could not afford one single slip up in the run-in.

In the light of what happened during that run-in, it is a miracle that Arsenal held on.

The trouble started around March. Things had been boiling up for weeks. Then Peter Storey failed to turn up for training for ten days and was suspended by the club.

A key member of the successful era, he'd spent most of the season filling in, playing in the Reserves, filling in again and generally losing touch with first-team football.

Angered by the ban, he said he would never play for the club again. Already we'd seen Mancini replace O'Leary at centre-half; Alex Cropley missed a long spell through injury, Radford came in as Frank Stapleton was moved back to the Reserves and Trevor Ross established himself in midfield – where Storey wanted to be.

Confusion and apathy reigned. In the end we held yet another noisy team meeting behind closed doors. This time we meant business. The players genuinely felt concerned by the apparent lack of interest being shown at managerial level. We decided to confront Bertie Mee.

Just when things were at their lowest ebb, Mee took us aback with a speech of Churchillian proportions.

In that measured, business-like tone of his, he made us feel guilty for ever challenging him on such a subject. As we shuffled our feet, Mee laid his feelings on the line. We were more important to him than anything. Arsenal was his life and his ideal finale would be to walk across the Highbury pitch one day and drop down dead.

By the time Mee had finished countering our accusation of neglect he had earned genuine applause from the players, who for the first time in many months, felt they had support and someone on their side.

A short time later, his Arsenal career ended!

On 22 March in front of surprised and embarrassed journalists, Bertie Mee wept as he announced his retirement at the end of the season. It was a reasonably decent way out for him, but we all knew that Arsenal wanted a new manager. And they had told Mee as much to his face.

This was the signal for an even more dramatic outburst, this time of something I had never seen before – player-power.

The players were split over who should become manager. The young brigade generally hoped for a completely new face. But we quickly discovered that a group of the seniors wanted Bobby Campbell to become manager the moment Mee vacated his office.

It was a weird situation because Mee was still the boss.

The back-room squabbles had their effect on the field. We lost 3–0 at Leeds United, 2–0 at home to Spurs and held on for a 0–0 at Everton.

Wolves came to Highbury on 13 April and both teams knew how important the game was.

We were seventeenth in the table, they were nineteenth, but while we were sliding, they had just beaten Newcastle 5–0 so their confidence was boosted. I scored, John Richards equalized before the break and they were, to be fair, bringing the best out of one of Arsenal's most consistent players that season, Jimmy Rimmer.

It was then that Terry Mancini scored his one and only goal for Arsenal and he couldn't have chosen a better time to do it – a header from a left wing corner. It won us both points. The significance? We stayed up, despite losing our last three games! Wolves went down.

The fans celebrated. The players did not. We were rocked when we discovered that Brian Kidd, Brian Hornsby and Eddie Kelly were all put on the transfer list.

Then the rumours began. Crack Yugoslavian coach Miljan Miljanic was, according to a *Daily Express* exclusive, 'having talks' with Arsenal.

I felt a strange mixture of elation and depression. The season was over. I had played in forty-one of the forty-two League games and knew that I had completed a successful season on a personal level.

I also knew that those other young lads who had broken through were on the threshold of achieving great things. Time, however, was not on our side. Success was wanted now, not in the future.

Arsenal seemed so sure of getting Miljanic that things were allowed to grind to a halt. Bertie went, and it all seemed so cold and business-like. Once again I was reminded that I am, after all, in business, big business, where promises of great things to come are usually not enough. Those great things are wanted immediately.

Mee, like so many managers, was unable to tell you the whole truth all the time. But he was always a fair man, and deserved a better farewell.

And with a club like Arsenal, rich enough to spend on good players, as indeed Mee's successor did, excuses are dismissed. The fact that Mee had introduced in 1975–76 the backbone of the FA Cup winners and title-chasers of 1979 and 1980, meant nothing up in that oak-panelled board-room where cigar smoke often constitutes the most tangible part of the atmosphere.

Down in the dressing-room, I was sick and tired of Campbell's increasing criticism, his repeated accusations that I was not pulling my weight, not contributing enough graft, not fulfilling my potential.

But the pressures on Campbell were enormous, and I have no doubt that they contributed to his change of attitude. I owe Campbell a lot, despite our rows.

Standing up to his criticism contributed to my growing up process. I knew what my family were going through. Dublin is the kind of city where people always want to be involved and have their say. I have heard it said that Dubliners are a fair breed . . . they give everybody stick.

When you are doing well, you can feel like a king. But god help you and your folks, if you are doing badly. Not that the remarks are malicious. But people want you and your family to know that they are in touch, that they understand, that they, too, are worried about the way things are going.

It all adds up to a strange type of unexpected pressure. Suddenly you feel accountable to thousands of people. In reality it is all very trivial. But when things are going wrong, such an awareness of responsibility can weigh a bit heavily.

Just when the prospect of a Yugoslavian manager seemed

73

likely, it all fell through and Arsenal were left high and dry.

The seniors seized their chance. We held a team meeting to sort out just how many of us were behind the group backing 'Campbell for manager'.

Alan Ball, George Armstrong and Terry Mancini were the leaders of the 'cause', but I, for one, disagreed. I still wanted a new face, a fresh influence on the scene.

Bally was disgusted with me. He even accused me of stabbing him in the back when I voted against the idea. Most of the young players did – Stapleton and Rostron were two – but because I had been such a 'Ball admirer' often hanging on his every word and listening to his undoubtedly sound advice, he expected me to back his cause.

Then I realized one of the great dangers to a young player – that of becoming so reliant on the assistance, advice and example of a top-class senior that his off-field influence can also affect your career.

I was adamant. But not all of the players were prepared to take one side or the other. In the end, including the abstentions, Bally's side won a vote by the narrowest possible margin.

Yet when he made his announcement to the world he said that Campbell had the full backing of all the players!

What none of us had taken into consideration was the fact that the board were totally uninterested in the opinions of a playing staff in whom they had long since lost confidence.

In their blinkered eyes, we were the cause of all the problems. All the same, were we not the players who came so close to taking their Arsenal into the Second Division? Were we not the players who compared so poorly with the side which swept the honours back in 1970 and 1971?

The hunt for a manager continued. Campbell, to be fair, kept his mouth shut and tried to maintain a degree of dignity. But it was difficult under the circumstances. He wanted the job. That was no secret. But the way in which Arsenal went about not giving it to him still leaves a bad taste in the mouth.

Big names hit the headlines. Dave Sexton was mentioned. Terry Venables was actually offered the job, but stunned the soccer world by turning down Arsenal because he had made a 'gentleman's agreement' with Palace chairman Ray Bloye.

Meanwhile Campbell struggled on, no doubt feeling more and more like a last resort, a situation which, at any level, cannot be acceptable.

Finally, Terry Neill was appointed – Campbell left and the new Arsenal took its first step out of the shadows of discontent.

Ahead lay big transfers, shock departures and arrivals and the dawning of a new, exciting and successful era. It, too, had its teething troubles, but the difference between good clubs and great clubs is that the great clubs always ride their temporary storms and come out on top.

7

New Manager, Old Problems

Terry Neill's achievements as Arsenal manager will go down in history, certainly the club's history, as irrefutable proof that his appointment as Bertie Mee's successor was a good one and a wise one. But history is unlikely to tell the whole story. Because the truth is that he struggled badly during his first season, made what I believe were wrong decisions concerning the players he sold, twice came close to facing a player-revolution as a direct result of his own actions and at one stage drove his players to the stage where they were forming a queue outside his office to present transfer requests.

I was one of those players. I'd had enough. I witnessed the gradual disintegration of a very good team before Neill's arrival and, like all the lads, looked to him to change things, to brighten our prospects as a club.

Far from improving the atmosphere at Highbury during that first season, it seemed to us that Neill made it worse. In some ways it was not his fault. But we felt he failed to grasp the importance of being straight with his staff. In the end it was my impression that most of the players were unable to take him at his word and we simply lost respect for the man.

This lack of respect was the sole reason for the way things came to a head during the club's close-season tour of Singapore and Australia. Faced with mounting, and at times blatant, disregard for his authority, Neill was forced to put his foot down. But even then he bungled it. He sent home two players as examples to the rest of us. He could have sent home seven or eight, including me.

Nobody at Arsenal visualized this type of situation before

season 1976–77 kicked-off. To us, the problems and discontent of the previous seasons were at last going to be solved. Change was necessary and, although we felt a lot of sympathy for Bertie Mee as he cleared out his office to make way for the new manager, we also felt a buzz of excitement all around the club.

Personally I was determined to play my part in making the team the best in the country. I was always very proud to be an Arsenal player, no matter what rows and misunderstandings littered my time at Highbury.

Through those mediocre seasons of change and rebuilding, I made good progress as a player. I became harder, more aware of my overall team responsibilities and, accepting Bally's advice, shouldered my share of responsibility on the field.

I became aware of the need to make things happen during a game. No longer was I partly looking to the seniors to lead before contributing my bit. Now I wanted to create things, force opponents to play the game our way, fight them for the upper hand.

All it needed really to spark things off was for somebody to come in and shake things up, bury the past and get the squad that we had working towards a common aim, a united style of play, and with confidence. That was an essential.

I spent that close-season summer reading the newspapers and attempting, without much success, to work out who would be there when I returned to Highbury.

There was talk of transfers galore. Deals were supposed to be going through, players being approached.

I expected to see this type of speculation. But it seemed that Arsenal were willing to approach a whole series of managers rather than give the job to Bobby Campbell. It was a miserable and unsettling time for Campbell. I know I took a lot of stick from him towards the end of the previous season, but I worked for him and I saw both sides of the situation. He wanted the job and said so openly. More and more, however, he realized that he was not going to get it.

People may wonder why the hell he wanted to stay with a club where the atmosphere was so unsettled. But when you consider the strong squad of players at Highbury at that time, it did not need a genius to see that all that was required was a spark – and some straight, hard talking – to produce a damn good team.

And this is where I believe we blundered, badly. By the end of that season, top-class players had gone. In fact nearly every link with the successful team of the early 1970s was broken.

To be fair, a lot of players were discontented and talking about leaving. But they did not have to leave. I am convinced that most of them would have been delighted to stay with Arsenal if the air had been cleared, if they could have seen some sign of a settled reign and strong leadership.

Jimmy Rimmer played consistently, and at times brilliantly, behind a defence which lacked nothing in skill and experience.

Pat Rice and Sammy Nelson were settled as the respective full-backs; David O'Leary was already an obvious star in the making and his partnership with Peter Simpson was well-balanced although injuries sometimes prevented them from playing together, and later Peter, or 'Stan' as he was nicknamed, departed.

Alan Ball, Eddie Kelly, George Armstrong, John Radford, Peter Storey, Alex Cropley, Brian Kidd, Frank Stapleton . . . a tremendous array of talent, eagerly chased by a Reserve side containing lads such as Graham Rix, David Price, John Matthews, Wilf Rostron, Ritchie Powling and Trevor Ross.

Many of those younger players had already made an impact in the First Division. It seemed only a matter of time before Arsenal could parade a superb side, backed up with strength in depth at Reserve level.

But when a new manager arrives at a club, he usually brings new ideas with him. And he usually prunes his squad, buying and selling in order to create 'his' team, playing 'his' football. Neill brought his assistant, Wilf Dixon, with him from Spurs. So it was no surprise to any of us when Campbell left the club a few days after Neill's July arrival.

I suppose from that moment, people like Ball, Armstrong, Mancini – the players who backed Campbell's campaign for the job – knew their time was limited. And so it proved.

Brian Kidd joined Manchester City a matter of days before Neill arrived, so it would be untrue to link that transfer with the new manager.

Equally, however, Neill received all the credit for the signing of Malcolm Macdonald from Newcastle United. But as we understood it, talks for Malcolm were going on before Neill came. In fact Bertie Mee and Gordon Clark were involved in that deal.

The first thing I noticed when Neill's appointment was announced was the reactions of those players who had played alongside him for Arsenal.

They were not at all happy about the prospect of working under a former team-mate, a situation which can cause all sorts of problems, not the least of which is the old saying linking familiarity with contempt!

The important thing, however, was the feeling of change. I began training with a squad that now had something to look forward to, a new challenge, new faces at the club. But we did not expect quite so many established faces to disappear before the season was over.

Macdonald arrived in a blaze of glory and publicity. His first message to London was: 'I will score thirty goals this season.' His brashness and larger-than-life personality shook the club in all the right ways.

I for one was delighted to see him arrive. His reputation for scoring goals was established. And by the end of the season he came within one goal of meeting that impressive target, scoring twenty-nine goals . . . and missing a penalty that would have made it thirty.

But Malcolm was also a selfish player. He was single-minded about his style of play and Neill, for one, was unable to change him.

We quickly realized that we would have to change our style of play to get that long, probing ball up to Malcolm and hope he stuck it away. For a while it worked. But when he dried up for a spell, our football suffered.

Our opening game of the season, minus me due to illness, was at home to Bristol City. More than 40,000 people turned up, but we flopped – the papers said Malcolm flopped, which was the type of pressure he brought on himself, but no, the team played badly – and City won 1–0.

John Radford, who opened the season alongside Malcolm,

was dropped after that one game. Frank Stapleton took the number 10 shirt, I was back in and Malcolm opened his Arsenal account in a 3–1 win at Norwich.

He scored again in a 2–2 draw at Sunderland, and by the time we beat Everton 3–1 at Highbury with goals from me, Frank and Malcolm, Arsenal stood third in the First Division table.

I was already experiencing a personal glow, but it had little to do with Arsenal's good start.

On 8 September 1976 I played in the game that had been on my mind since my childhood in Dublin. Ireland played England at Wembley and for the first time in my life I felt a type of nervous anxiety that I would not wish on my worst enemy.

David O'Leary and I were the Arsenal members of an Ireland team that was unquestionably one of the best to come out of the country in the Republic's history.

We had played together in a number of matches over a short period of time and we were full of running, confidence and belief in our own ability.

England, if anything, were in the opposite frame of mind. Don Revie's side was struggling to produce the standard of football the English fans expected and Revie even warned his players not to underestimate us on the night.

The result which worried Revie was our 2–0 victory over the full Polish side in Poznan that May. We played some marvellous football in Poland and the world's press gave us full credit.

Yet only another Irishman could understand the type of pressure we were under before the England game. Dublin was so excited by the game that I don't think many other topics of conversation were discussed throughout the city.

Above all else, we wanted to give our country a performance of which they could be proud. We not only achieved that aim, but came close to beating England on their own top stage.

The game was my first at Wembley. I was told what to expect, the atmosphere, the sheer size of the place; John Giles was no stranger there and he made sure that we were prepared.

What he did not expect was to discover that there seemed to be more Irish fans than English fans in the stadium.

Giles was outstanding on the night. He pulled the game our way and we played a creative, studied type of football, more the style people expect from Continental sides.

England struggled to get possession and I remember thinking how devastated they would be if we could stick just one goal past Ray Clemence. You could sense that the England side was anxious.

Ironically, Stuart Pearson somehow deflected a ball from the right inside Mike Kearns' near post to give England the lead, and most neutrals expected us to break out and go at them, forgetting all our carefully laid plans.

The England triumph did not materialize because we did not abandon our plans. We continued building carefully, using the ball from midfield and producing sudden changes of pace near the England area.

We really should have scored before Gerry Daly equalized from the penalty spot, and we should have wrapped it up after that.

But I believe that the Ireland team announced its arrival as a potential international force that night. Other countries at last looked upon us as a team meriting respect.

Once again I returned to Arsenal, aware of the difference between a collection of happy players and a divided camp.

I was disappointed when I learned that Eddie Kelly had joined QPR. It was a waste because after a short spell of success there, he faded out of the top-class game. If Eddie had stayed with Arsenal and buckled down to the job he would probably have shared the great days that were destined to unfold from the situation he left.

Pat Howard joined us from Newcastle. We needed strengthening at the centre of the defence, and Paddy seemed to be the player to fill the gap. His friendship with Malcolm helped swing the deal.

He played for a while alongside David O'Leary, but when Neill signed Willie Young from Spurs, it spelt the beginning of the end for Pat, and he knew it. Neill signed Howard, then seemed to forget him, an attitude none of the players could understand. Given the chance, Pat could have settled in London, but he eventually left and joined Birmingham City.

Results were good and we battled through to the League Cup fourth round after a three-match scrap with Blackpool. But off the field things were deteriorating again. And this time I was involved and I was growing fed up with the whole boring situation.

Ball and Neill did not get on. It was as simple as that. And when Bally began picking Neill up on some of the things he came out with concerning tactics and discipline, we all knew that it could not last.

Then they had a couple of real rows, with Bally delivering what he believed to be a series of home truths to his manager. It was obvious that something had to give.

Things reached the stage where half the team sided with Neill and the other half with Ball. And that is a situation which cannot exist. Incredibly, it existed at Arsenal for nearly half a season.

One by one the squad broke up. Little Alex Cropley joined Aston Villa and Terry Mancini went to Aldershot. Terry had done a good job for the club during his stay, but he was a Campbell signing and knew his career was better served elsewhere. But Alex was simply too brave for his own good. Built like a kite-frame, he tackled like a bulldozer and spent more time injured than he did playing.

We all admired Alex for his tremendous courage and grit. But even at Villa he could not change his style. And injuries have dogged him at Villa Park.

Graham Rix was coming through in the Reserves and Bally repeatedly expressed the opinion that 'This boy is a natural, he will soon take the game by storm'.

But Alex had the experience while Graham's skill was still unsupported by professional know-how. We had lost another class player, and it was too soon to use Graham Rix to fill the gap.

Ireland lost a controversial match 2–0 to France in Paris, in a very important World Cup qualifying tie. We dominated the first half, gave away a stupid goal, saw what I still believe to be a perfectly legitimate equalizer ruled out and then let in another goal.

This was a genuine setback to our World Cup hopes. We saw

the group as a great chance of qualifying for the first time, and I confess to having felt really depressed with the way things seemed to be going on all fronts.

It was, of course, a premature reaction. But Arsenal was once again an unhappy place to be. In the December I saw two good friends leave the club. John Radford went to West Ham and Bally was transferred to Southampton.

For the first time in my career I considered the possibility of getting away from this whole mad human supermarket. The seeds were sown for a transfer request.

Pat Rice became team captain when Alan Ball left and we got behind him straight away. But results spluttered. We were reaping the rewards of selling the wrong players.

Yet it all seemed so crazy. We'd beaten Chelsea 2–1 in a thrilling League Cup fourth round tie in front of 52,000 fans in October. The supporters were behind us, believing that a new era was dawning.

Ironically they were right. A new era was close at hand. But few of the players, if any, could see it. All we knew was that the season was slipping away from us and, it seemed to us at the time, Neill was not going to inspire the respect and authority we thought the whole place needed to get the team on the rails.

The whole stupid situation was summed up that December when Frank McLintock and Eddie Kelly inspired QPR to a 2–1 League Cup fifth round victory over us at Loftus Road.

Just seeing them on the 'other side' was enough to remind all of us of the mistakes that had been made while the team was being dismantled.

In many ways, Alan Ball did not have to leave Highbury. But in others he most definitely did. His battle with Terry Neill was always going to be a loser. Because Neill knew that, as manager, he had to act or lose all respect.

So Ball went. Neill stayed. Arsenal suffered the loss of a great player. It was a genuine tragedy. I take it as fact that such a situation must always come out on the manager's side because he has the responsibility and the authority. To allow it to be repeatedly challenged – as was happening in Ball's case – is to lose the job altogether in the long run.

Nevertheless, the balance of comings and goings was now

beyond a joke. We were worried because the team was suffering a gradual bleeding of talent.

So when Neill signed Alan Hudson, a player of undoubted pedigree, from Stoke after that Christmas, his arrival was greeted with genuine enthusiasm.

I envisaged a great midfield combination with 'Huddy' giving us the right-sided stability. It was not to be. Why? Because of more personality clashes.

It was bad enough that the man Neill sold, Alan Ball, went because of repeated arguments. But when we discovered that Neill and the man he had bought, Alan Hudson, were also at immediate loggerheads, we could not believe it.

Hudson came to Highbury with a reputation for being a bit of a problem-player. He also came with a reputation as one of the most gifted footballers in the country.

For some reason best known to themselves, Arsenal, through Neill, persuaded Hudson to move into a house quickly. I suppose they feared the worst if they failed to get him settled down as soon as he arrived.

But Huddy had house problems of his own. He wanted to do things his own way. In the end it proved the spark that flamed into a row with Hudson declaring: 'I will never play for that man again.'

Great! The outgoing players were unhappy. The incoming players were unhappy. The rest of us, well, we just shook our heads and asked when it was all going to end.

8

Breaking Point

Bad weather began to hit the League programme midway through the season, but we managed to pick up some form and climbed back from thirteenth to sixth in the First Division table.

But our revival must have given our supporters a very false impression of what things were like behind the scenes. As we moved up the table, the fans must have imagined a good and strong dressing-room spirit off-stage.

If only they had known. I sensed a definite lack of conviction on the part of most of the side. It was as if we were all waiting for the bubble to burst, but nobody wanted to be the prophet of gloom and say as much openly.

The team was playing to Malcolm's strengths, and while Frank Stapleton deserves credit for the rapid strides he made at this time, we lacked top-quality cover in too many departments. And what was worse, too many senior players did not respect Terry Neill sufficiently to give us any hope of overcoming the lean spell which seemed almost inevitably to be waiting around the corner.

Although none of us wanted things to deteriorate, it was as if we were all giving off the same silent signals of anxiety bordering on despair.

We all sensed that things needed attending to, but nobody actually spoke up, a factor which undoubtedly led to a deepening of depression all round.

Malcolm scored some stunning goals, and without doubt lived up to his boast and his reputation. But we did play to him too much, at the expense of putting to better use the alternative weapons the side possessed.

When he struggled, the whole team struggled. And that should not have been the case. The team possessed a lot of good players. But the way we were playing concentrated on Malcolm's game more than that of any other member of the team.

Terry lacked nothing in enthusiasm. But it was more and more evident that he needed the support of a good, strong, coach. Our work during the week simply did not produce the necessary variation nor the inspiration to improve the team.

And, of course, there was that nagging element of discomfort felt by those players who had known Terry Neill as a teammate. They knew him too well, knew his character and therefore he could not present a new face to them. It was impossible for him to introduce something into the situation which would have made those players think: 'Wait a minute, I thought I knew this guy, but there are more sides to him than I realized.'

In reality there were not more sides to the man. He was enthusiastic and ambitious and genuinely anxious for the team to improve and do well. But he was also unpredictable and often left me with the feeling that I did not know him at all and that my question of the moment had not in fact been answered but rather side-stepped.

I say that nobody wanted to speak up. But Bally did just that. The problem was that he went to the other extreme and we witnessed some strong rows between Neill and Ball, rows that, as I said, hastened Ball's departure from Highbury.

January brought a New Year and, it was hoped, a fresh challenge. The FA Cup third round draw took us to Meadow Lane where a second-half goal by Trevor Ross proved enough to beat Notts County.

Alan Hudson's graceful skills were definitely adding to our team-play, and when we beat Norwich City 1–0 at home the following week it lifted us into fourth place in the First Division.

Hudson's ability was breathtaking. At his best he was undoubtedly one of the best midfield players in the game and really should have won many more caps for England than the few his talents actually earned.

Essentially a right-sided player, Huddy glided gracefully

through tackles and left opponents sitting on their backsides simply by shifting his stance over the ball. It was exciting to watch him play and equally exciting to be in the same team with him.

His passing was superb. Huddy picked out players in a flash and dropped the ball precisely into their paths or to their feet, depending on the situation. He would then race into a supporting position so that he could receive the ball again or create space for the man in possession.

This type of ability cannot be manufactured. Huddy was born with his talent and it is football's loss that the game did not see more of him at the very top level.

For a while, things went well. In fact I stopped worrying and began to believe in the way the team was playing.

Malcolm was at his deadly best in the fourth round tie against Coventry City at Highbury at the end of January. His two goals, plus one from Frank Stapleton, gave us a 3–1 win and suddenly, we were together, a team with somewhere to go. But we suspected that the cracks were being plastered over instead of being repaired.

Ironically, as things brightened at Arsenal they darkened on the international front.

Spain beat us 1–0 in Dublin and became the first nation to win there since October 1972.

With the France disappointment still fresh in their minds, the Irish supporters started to give us stick – something I had not experienced before.

It felt strange to return to London and look forward to rejoining the Arsenal squad. How often that situation had been reversed. Now it was the turn of the Irish squad to feel the pressure.

But the big difference was Giles. The squad remained close and united. We took things in our stride and Giles made this possible through his leadership and positive example. Ireland was developing as an international team. We all knew it and Giles was not afraid to remind us.

How could I have guessed what fate held in store for all of us?

From fourth in the table and FA Cup fifth round qualifiers, our world crashed around us.

87

Pat Rice's winner against Norwich proved to be the last winning goal to be scored by any Arsenal player for an unprecedented eleven First Division matches on the trot!

That fourth round win over Coventry was the only bright spot in a nightmare run during which we slumped down to a meaningless mid-table position and took a real fifth-round hammering off Middlesbrough.

As I feared, when Malcolm dried up, as he did for a spell, the whole team suddenly appeared to function on three cylinders. We did not utilize the strength in the side sufficiently, and paid the penalty.

It was not Malcolm's fault. The team was geared to play to him. But after a promising first few games, when his skill was evident, Huddy stopped producing the form expected of him. His battle with Neill was partly responsible for his sluggish form, as was his continued domestic upheaval concerning houses.

My form dipped as well. Maybe we all began to try too hard. But, whatever the reason, things went from bad to worse. And just when we needed him most, Neill let us down.

I believe that one of the signs of a great manager is his ability to obtain the respect of his players, and to be able to hammer those players within the confidential walls of the club when they let him down, without letting them down or attacking them through the media.

For some strange reason, best known to himself, Neill chose to adopt the very opposite approach, and his behaviour disgusted and embittered the vast majority of his squad.

We played away to Middlesbrough on 13 February, played very badly and took a 3–0 hammering which could, with better finishing on their part, have been considerably worse. No excuses – we just did not touch our capabilities and expected a justified rocket when we came off.

But to our amazement, Neill shook his head and mumbled something about the performance not being good enough. That, to put it mildly, was an understatement. Now players know when they deserve a telling-off. We certainly did after that game. We also needed some kind of booster, something to clear the air and get us all talking about what went wrong.

Just when we thought that Neill had decided to play the whole thing down, we read in the next day's papers how he had supposedly roasted us after the game. And Neill was quoted as saying: 'This was the worst Arsenal performance since I took over as manager. We could not have beaten eleven dustbins on that display.'

I am not sure if he was attempting to be funny or just having a go. But I do know that the players felt let down, angry and even less trusting than before. It was a silly and ever-deteriorating problem.

Some of the lads ended up having rows with him over his remarks, and his unpredictable way of doing things. Not one of us would have opened our mouths if he had torn that dressing room apart and really taken us to task for the way we lost to 'Boro. But Neill was wrong to ignore his players, attack them in the press, then leave them to find out what he really thought through their local newsagent.

This is where it becomes possible to make the comparison between the top manager and the rest. Unfortunately, in this respect, I believe Neill belongs with 'the rest'.

When I talk of great managers, I immediately think of Sir Alf Ramsey, Matt Busby, Bill Shankly, Bob Paisley, Dave Sexton, Don Revie, Jock Stein and John Giles. I am sure that among this list there are men who are not exactly every football person's cup of tea. But they all have one great strength in common – the ability to command respect.

To the outside world this respect comes as a result of tangible successes in the major competitions – the winning of League Championships and Cups.

But to the professional footballers, leadership and honesty rate just as highly as inspired tactical knowledge.

Players talk among themselves when they meet, either socially or after a game, and I know for a fact that every one of the managers I have named is capable of reading the riot act to a whole dressing-room full of players, or to an individual, depending on which he deems necessary.

They can be very hard men indeed, men who have no time for players who are not prepared to give 100 per cent and have no qualms about telling players exactly that. But it is their players that they tell . . . not the media!

When Ramsey emerged from the dressing-room after England's 1–1 World Cup draw with Poland, a result which ended their hopes of qualifying, he told the world that his players had been 'magnificent' and backed them to the hilt. Yet he might well have prolonged his career as England manager if he had, for once, laid some blame for the overall failure at their door. But that was not Ramsey's way. Whatever he said to those players afterwards was between him and them. And for that reason alone, players were prepared to follow him, over a cliff if necessary.

Anyone who believes that Shankly spent his whole career making witty remarks or that Busby always treated players like a wise old uncle, is living in dream land.

Revie's public support for his players, even during their most bitterly disappointing last-gasp failures, gave the impression that he possessed the patience of a saint. But make no mistake. He made his feelings known behind locked doors when he thought it necessary.

No matter how much criticism a manager directs towards a player, that player will take it and be able to cope . . . as long as he does not have to cope with his problems being splashed across national newspaper sports pages.

This is where Neill went wrong. He fell down on this basic necessity, the ability to convince his players of his loyalty to them. There is not much of this particular commodity in football anyway. But when it comes to the day-to-day relationship between one man and a large collection of individuals, a basic loyalty is essential. Neill did not show it. Therefore he did not receive it.

To make matters worse, Gordon Clark left the club because of personal differences with Terry Neill, and to lose a man of Gordon's talent was absurd. Here was a top scout, whose work had produced something in the region of £2 million for Arsenal, being allowed to drift off because of yet another personality clash.

As if things were not bad enough, we went back to play 'Boro in the fifth round of the Cup and lost 4–1, David Mills scoring a hat-trick.

Our run became so bad that we equalled, and eventually beat, the previous Arsenal all-time failure record of six consecutive defeats, a record that had stood for fifty-two years!

The team talks became a joke, a series of squabbles and niggles, most of them stemming from a lack of confidence in Terry.

This is no whitewash. The team was off-form to such a degree that we were worried about where the next win was coming from. If he had managed to make us believe that he had one moment of genuine concern and application we would have backed the man to his tracksuit top.

Far from giving us reason to rally round, Neill repeated his 'dustbins' attack, only this time he went too far and came as close as any manager has ever come to watching a whole team walk out on him.

We played at home to Ipswich and were trounced 4–1. Nobody needed to be told how bad we were, although to be fair we were not enjoying a lot of luck either. That is often the way it goes in football.

This is when you need support. This is when players, especially young players, look to their manager and all but yell 'please tell us what the hell is going wrong'.

We did not have that type of leadership. I have no doubt at all that Terry Neill was doing his best. I don't say for one moment that he did not care, because he most certainly did.

But whereas all people look good when things are going OK, you only see what a person is really made of when things go wrong. You see how they cope with a crisis and make your overall judgement from that.

I think Terry panicked. He was not able to instil in us the confidence that he was armed with the know-how to cope, or that he possessed the technical knowledge to take hold of the whole team, shake the hell out of it and make necessary changes.

What he did do was astonishing. He said nothing to us, then went out and described us on TV as 'morons'.

If ever a remark was calculated to cause trouble, that was it. And when he heard and saw it on the box, I think Neill realized he had gone too far. He seemed half afraid to face us on the Monday morning.

91

I was so bloody angry that I was prepared to confront him and demand that in future he was to say what he had to say to our faces. Deep down, however, I was coming to the conclusion that as far as Arsenal and me were concerned, there was not going to be any future.

We lost our next two games as well, at home to West Bromwich Albion and away to QPR before ending the rot with a 1–1 draw up at Stoke.

Even then the game was marred when I was sent off after a flare-up involving Tony Waddington's son, Steve. I deserved to go for retaliating, but I think a lot of it was deep-rooted frustration at another season wasted.

I was fed up, George Armstrong was rowing with Neill more and more, Huddy was unsettled and off-form, Peter Storey went the way of the rest of the 'double' side when he was transferred, in his case to Fulham.

Turning full circle, my emotions were once again at their highest when we played France in Dublin in the World Cup 'return' fixture.

We all knew that we had to win. There was no other way of keeping ourselves involved in the World Cup qualifying battle. And the Irish fans, their disappointment long forgotten, packed Lansdowne Road on 30 March.

The 48,000 crowd never let up and partly deafened the French into submission. It was a memorable match and without doubt the highlight of my season.

The French, destined to make such a wonderful impression in Argentina during the World Cup, were underestimated in Europe, and to a certain extent probably still are. They gave us a good game in Dublin with players such as Bathenay, Platini, Lacombe and Rocheteau displaying their skills and technique. We all realized the importance of the game and a tremendous team effort saw us through. And I was thrilled to score our goal early in the first half. It was enough to give us two points and leave both nations looking across the Iron Curtain at Bulgaria, the third team in Group Five.

2 April saw us beat Leicester 3–0 at Highbury. The result was badly needed, our first League win since January. But the real significance of the result lay in the

goal-scorers on the day.

Graham Rix, playing his first League match for the club, made it a scoring debut and David O'Leary stormed forward from the back to score twice – the first League goals of his professional career.

Two players destined to play a major role in a much happier and more successful era made their first real headlines. It was something few people inside the club realized until some time afterwards.

There was one hell of a team at Arsenal fighting to get its head above the squabbles and misunderstandings. That team was just a season away. But at the time it seemed an unlikely outcome.

Then, as if nothing had happened, we began to get our game together again. The football was more relaxed, the bad run ended – we just put it behind us and built on the Leicester result for what remained of the season.

From being shaky and brittle, the defence tightened up to such an extent that we conceded only two goals in a great run of eight matches.

It made us wonder what we might have achieved that season if we had not collapsed so alarmingly half-way.

I believe that the introduction of John Matthews in midfield was a contributory factor. His work-rate was good and he really had something to prove to Terry Neill. John wanted a regular place, as does every youngster, and when given his chance, he fought to make the most of it.

Alan Hudson turned on some class displays for us in the wins over Spurs, Coventry, Villa and Newcastle. Yet it all seemed so much so late, too late to matter a damn. We were not high enough in the table to qualify for Europe – something I wanted badly to experience – and finished eighth.

Most of us knew that 'Geordie' Armstrong was totally fed up with his personal battle with Terry Neill. What we did not know was that Armstrong's appearance in an Arsenal shirt in our final game of the season, against Manchester United at Old Trafford, was his last competitive match for the club.

World Cup action took me out to Bulgaria with Ireland in the June. But our lousy away fortunes continued as the

Bulgarians squeezed home by 2–1 despite a goal by Don Givens. We felt we were cheated and robbed in this game. Giles scored a perfectly good goal which was disallowed for no visible reason, and we all felt sick at losing in such a dubious manner.

It was heartbreaking, really, because a draw out in Sofia, which we came so close to getting, would have put us in a great position.

Meanwhile Arsenal were preparing for a tour of the Far East which was destined to end in controversy.

The problems of the season were not lost on the board, who realized that something had to be done. What was obvious was that Neill required a top-class coach who would leave him with the manager's tasks minus the bulk of the coaching.

Before long it became common knowledge that Arsenal were on the hunt for a top man. Miljanic's name came up yet again. Dave Sexton, who had resigned as manager of QPR, was on the verge of joining Arsenal when Manchester United stepped in and offered him the job of manager.

Sexton eventually chose Old Trafford and our tour began with nothing resolved.

There was, however, something which I had resolved – to get away from Highbury. Enough, in my opinion, was enough. I could not see anything ahead except another season of battling away in an atmosphere more changeable than the weather. I'd seen friends sold, top-class players sold, and knew that more were keen to get away. I decided to join the exodus.

My transfer request came as a shock to Neill, but I was adamant and it was put before the board. I decided to take my time after that and just see what developed.

Without wishing to appear conceited, I knew that even at twenty-one, my reputation was such that there would not be a shortage of clubs interested if Arsenal decided to let me go.

My only concern was that they might put a daft fee on my head and create some kind of long drawn-out saga. In fact it never came to that.

We jetted out to the Far East, playing a couple of games in the woeful humidity of Singapore, before arriving in Australia. There we were due to take part in a four-team tournament that also involved Celtic, Red Star Belgrade and the Australian national side.

But it was not the football that proved the talking point of that ill-fated trip. More and more it became obvious that a lack of basic respect for Terry Neill was being displayed by the senior players who took less and less notice of his orders.

Not that anybody went beyond the limits of common sense. It was purely a matter of internal concern.

Drinking was at the hub of the matter and, although he tried to ignore it as much as possible, Neill was forced to act when Malcolm and Huddy were seen drinking the day before a game by officials, including chairman Denis Hill-Wood.

We expected things to come to a head. Not that I defend our behaviour because I simply cannot. It was wrong to go about things the way we did. But, in a perverse sort of way, our behaviour proved our point. Because Neill promptly told Malcolm and Huddy that they were being sent home – alone.

Now this was nothing more than an attempt to make it look as if he had control of the situation and knew how to crack down in the proper managerial fashion.

The truth is that I should have gone with them, Geordie Armstrong demanded to be let go with them and the whole squad was in uproar. Matters had only been made worse.

The really stupid thing was that they were sent home the day before the rest of us were due to fly back. I couldn't see the sense in this, but they were expelled from the tour, an act which guaranteed a troubled start to the next season as well.

9

The Way Clubs Treat
Players

When a youngster leaves his home to join a football club, he does so hoping that he is going from one family atmosphere to another. He looks for security, for warmth and trust, confidence-building discipline and basic fair-play and justice.

But while clubs do take steps to ensure that the young lads they sign are looked after, properly coached and trained to become professionals, there exists a definite attitude that players are cogs in a machine and therefore dispensable.

Over the years, the Victorian restrictions concerning freedom of speech, the right to choose your own place of employment, wage limitations and contract negotiations have all taken a battering. After years of serf-like conditions, the players gradually fought for, and won, many basic rights which are afforded to every other working person outside the game.

These triumphs, however, have done nothing to heal the rift between club and player. Every week we read about another internal battle – often triangular – involving directors of a club, the manager and a player. I believe that a basic lack of trust is to blame for a lot of the problems.

From the moment I came in contact with the professional game and sat down for my first discussions about a contract, I began to notice that the whole business operates on two levels.

Clubs do not inform players of all the ins and outs of contracts. They do not allow an agent to be present when you are negotiating. And I, for one, always came away feeling less than 100 per cent happy with the terms offered and equally unhappy with the nagging feeling that my employers had not laid all their cards on the table.

The average teenager will be confused and almost grateful to get his name down on a contract by the time he has come in contact with the business-side of his profession. I believe that clubs should be more honest with their players by spelling out exactly what they have in mind long-term. But then the whole game is so unpredictable – from the level of chairman down to the rawest recruit – that this is very difficult to do.

Why is it unpredictable? In my opinion because there are two sets of rules, one for the club and one for the players.

The moment a player asserts himself, asks questions and causes any kind of fuss over his working conditions and salary, he is looked upon as a trouble-maker or certainly a potential trouble-maker. You can sense it in the way directors look at you.

And in a society where the trade union movement is powerful and influential and where individuals have the right to question their standards of living and their income, it seems unfair that the footballer should be branded as a money-grabber when he dares to bring his fist down on somebody's desk.

Of course there are exceptions. Within the League there are good clubs and bad when it comes to handling players. Arsenal happen to be one of the better clubs. But that does not mean that I was totally happy with the way I was treated at Highbury, nor by the way the club treated other players during my time there.

Contracts are one big problem. In fact they have become so complicated that many players, me included, bring along a solicitor for any negotiations. This is simply a business-like way of doing things. But it also makes you all the more aware of the gap that exists. When it comes to the subject of cash, you do not belong to a caring, protective organization. You are employed by a business which in terms of comparison with other business giants, can be ruthless, cruel and totally money-orientated.

I have seen countless young boys discarded while still teenagers, all their hopes and dreams in ruins. But worse, their futures uncertain and their educations rarely completed. Too few of the teenage rejects go out of the game armed with a skill or training to provide them with a secure living.

Clubs do, in fairness, encourage their youngsters to study for a second trade or profession. Not only because it will guarantee them a job if they fail to make the grade, but also because the most successful career can be cut short through injury, and a married player with a family needs something to fall back on if he is told that he can no longer play at the professional level.

But encouraging players is one thing. Taking an active and parent-like involvement is another. Lots of lads come into football and are so wrapped up with the glamour and excitement of it all that it is impossible to get them to sit down twice a week and actually study. Only when it is too late do many of them see what an important thing an education is, even to a budding George Best.

Putting your finger on the overall problem is difficult. But it seems as if some old-world ideas rule at board-room level. They are the club. You are only the players. These people seem to forget that supporters spend their hard-earned money to watch the players, not the directors.

Without players, clubs would not exist. Yet there is always the strange attitude in the air that you should be grateful for being afforded the opportunity to come into the game, grateful for all the facilities laid on, grateful for being shown parts of the world you otherwise might never have seen.

Certainly the game opens up a whole new world to every young lad who comes into it. But foreign trips are usually made with financial reasons in mind, as indeed is everything a club does.

One of the most disturbing things about the club-player relationship involves the all-important third-party, the supporters.

I know for a fact that many people outside the game believe professional players to be greedy, spoiled and ungrateful. They think we are blinkered grabbers, constantly causing problems for the poor old directors while they put their backs into keeping their club afloat.

Naturally, not all players are angels. You find a cross-section of people in all walks of life. The average pro is a hard-working guy, ambitious, aware of his limitations and in love with the game.

He is also probably married. He may have a family for whom he has to provide security . . . long-term.

Yet his job is one which guarantees him absolutely nothing while promising him everything a young man can dream of. For between ten and thirteen years he knows that he can earn a good living providing he gets the right breaks, that his face fits and his manager likes him and that injuries do not cut him down.

There are a hell of a lot of 'ifs' in the job. And when a player's years are up and his body can no longer perform, he knows that there are struggles ahead if he has failed to get the best possible contracts for himself during his career.

This is where clubs do not treat players the way I believe they should. This is probably the most important area of all from a player's point of view . . . yet it is the most insecure and worrying.

The professional footballer does his job knowing that, unlike the vast majority of men, his career has a definite limit and usually ends at an age when other men are reaching their professional peak.

It is nothing short of tragic to read about some of the former great players ending up on street corners selling newspapers, struggling on the dole or scratching out a living simply because when they were providing top-class entertainment for thousands of people, week after week, their clubs did not have to pay them more than £20 a week.

There was uproar when Jimmy Hill did his bit to end the maximum wage. And there was uproar when the so-called 'Freedom of Contract' was introduced. Why? Because those Victorian restrictions were being removed. Clubs discovered that they could no longer call in a player whose contract had ended and tell him that they were going to slap a farcical fee on his head.

Over the years the resentment has grown, the mistrust festered. A player knows that the most attractive promises made to him count for nothing if the board makes an overnight decision to sack their manager.

The security is simply not there and a contract is, in many cases, just a piece of paper.

Just when a man believes he has arrived at the club with whom he will complete his career and fulfil his ambitions, the man who signed him and promised him all these things may be dismissed. A new manager arrives and more often than not brings his own back-room staff with him. Then he begins examining his squad.

If he happens to like a different type of player, one man's dreams of security in exchange for giving the club his very best can be shattered. He can be called in and told that he is up for sale. Just like a prize heffer.

The newspapers note the fact with a story of varying size depending on the player's reputation. But neither they nor the club really understand the anguish such bloody coups create.

The player has probably completed weeks of exhausting house hunting, often operating from some impersonal hotel room while his wife and children wait at home in the town where his previous club was located.

He and his wife then have the problem of moving their child or children to a new school. His whole family must tear up roots when he signs for a new club. And the roots have to be jerked up again if he is resold.

At what stage in his life does the pro really feel secure and able to face his family to guarantee them security? If you are waiting for an answer, I for one cannot provide it.

To establish real security, you have to have loyalty, on both sides. From club towards player and vice versa.

There is no loyalty as such. The game at the top level is business more than sport as far as clubs are concerned. The same contract that the player must fulfil can be torn up at a board-room whim if they decide to sell him; if he becomes something which will make them more money now than if they uphold the contract and keep the player until it expires.

I learned a hard lesson that season when I fell ill before a South East Counties League Cup Final. Even at that age the club preferred to accuse me of deliberately trying to avoid playing rather than take the trouble to find out the truth. As I have already said, it almost turned me against the game for good.

But the frightening aspect of that situation is the realization

100

that they suspected me quite naturally. Not because it was me, but because I was a player and therefore, in their eyes, probably more likely to be trying to 'swing the lead' a bit.

And then later, when Bertie Mee considered it quite within his rights to discuss my international career with John Giles and refuse Giles permission to take me on a South American tour . . . without even consulting me or telling me a straight 'No'.

This type of thing happens all the time. And it is wrong. In any other job there would be hell to pay if employers treated employees in such an off-hand fashion.

The question of loyalty is one which amazes me. Why? Because clubs simply cannot see that they discourage it at every turn.

In my case I found out the hard way. Because I joined the club from the beginning of my career, I was looked upon as almost part of the furniture. This is commonplace with youngsters who graduate up through the ranks and into the first team.

You see if the club goes out and buys a player for a large sum of money, the player knows that the club want him. So he is immediately put in a strong position when the time comes to talk business.

He can fight the terms if he believes them to be unjust or simply not enough, and do so knowing that, if the club has gone out of its way to get him there in the first place, it will do more to keep him happy than it would do for a lad who began his career with the club.

When I went to discuss contract problems with Arsenal I discovered that this attitude prevailed. I was, all the same, a part of the set-up. And was I not grateful for the fact that the club had given me my big chance, pushed me into the League game as a teenager? And so on.

It dawned on me that only when I left Arsenal, and joined another club who were prepared to spend money to get me, would I be in the ideal bargaining position. And if that is not a stupid situation, then I find it difficult to name one.

One might argue that in the end, you are better off hopping from club to club like a mercenary, not actually asking for a move but making it clear that you would not be unhappy about the idea.

So where the hell does loyalty come into the game? Only loyalty to yourself and your family. That is what the young player has to know and accept from the start. And naïve ideas about believing the sentimental drivel churned out by the media concerning 'happy, close-knit clubs' and 'one big happy family under so-and-so' need to be squashed from the outset.

Sadly, 'happy families' usually disintegrate the moment so-and-so gets the board-room chop.

In my case I came up against the classic example of disregard for a player and his feelings.

Denis Hill-Wood told the world that there was no way Arsenal would let me go and that I would become the highest paid player in the League if that's what it took to keep me at Highbury. I remember those words. He uttered them after we had beaten Manchester United in the 1979 FA Cup Final.

I remembered them again some months later when the same man was quoted in the national press as saying: 'We have given up all hope of keeping Liam Brady at this club.'

He found it necessary to tell the rest of Britain, but could not find the time to call me in first and let me in on the big decision! The first I knew about the club adopting this attitude was when I read it in the papers.

In a way I was glad, because it helped me to put things into perspective. I came to terms with the fact that I was an Arsenal player, not an Arsenal person. I was a business commodity. And it began to dawn on the club that they would make a lot more money out of me by selling me before my contract expired. Because then I would be free to decide my own future and there exists a financial limit to what a club may receive under those circumstances.

Certainly I have a strong feeling for Arsenal. That is inevitable. But it is never going to be so strong that it distorts my judgement.

They saw Graham Rix coming through, a player very similar in style to myself. They knew that I wanted to experience the game abroad. Yes, I was attracted by the financial rewards. But that was not my only reason for going. I was also itching to make the break and try something new. Few people understood this, but Kevin Keegan admits that he suffered from the same problem.

A true story Kevin relates sums up both our situations. He was waiting in an hotel lobby in London with some other players when a big Liverpool fan walked up and began telling Kevin how he had once admired him, but now thought nothing of him because he was going abroad just for 'more money'.

Kevin swallowed all the guy's complaints and the conversation turned to Liverpool, the atmosphere and the city's unique attraction. And without knowing the significance of what he was saying, the big Scouse admitted: 'I love the place and the club, but I don't live there any more.' When Kevin asked him why not he replied: 'My job. There is much more money to be earned in London.'

Yes, it was OK for him to seek a better living somewhere else, but not OK for K. Keegan, professional footballer. He is considered public property first and an individual second.

But getting back to Arsenal, I remember people coming up to me, directors and club officials, declaring their support for the cause of keeping me at Highbury. Those same men were doubtless around when it was decided to give up trying and let me go.

It is just as well that I did not adopt the attitude that I wanted to stay at Arsenal for life. Especially after picking up another national newspaper the day we were due to fly out to East Germany for a Cup Winners' Cup tie and reading: 'It would not be the end of the world if Liam Brady did leave this club. We would survive.' Who was talking? None other than my manager, Terry Neill. I would have liked him to tell me first or at least express those opinions to my face. Because whenever we did talk he gave me a very different impression.

The fans obviously believed that I let them down by leaving Arsenal. But I was around when two of the game's most respected, consistent and loyal pros received the full force of this game's ingratitude.

Even worse, I was partly involved when Arsenal decided to give us all an example of how they dispense justice, and it was an example that sickened me to such a degree that I almost told them where to stick their famous old club!

Arsenal Reserves travelled down to Cardiff and won by a large, convincing score. We were tremendously pleased with ourselves and with good reason.

Brendan Batson and Dave Donaldson, however, overdid their celebrations to the point where they committed an indiscretion.

I was not involved in their escapade. But I was a friend of Dave's, whose family had kindly agreed to put me up following the death of my landlord Mr Rowland. Understandably, Mrs Rowland and her son wanted to move out of the area, and the Donaldson family came to my rescue.

Dave and Brendan knew that they were on the carpet. But nobody expected the extraordinary decision Arsenal reached.

They obviously weighed up which player would make the grade at Highbury and which, if either, would not. Dave, it was decided, was less likely to make it than Brendan, so they kicked out Dave and Brendan stayed on!

How's that for logical justice? A decision that had nothing to do with fair play and everything to do with long-term business and using a human being, a young and impressionable Reserve, as an example to the rest.

Arsenal had no idea how much agony they caused through that decision. I felt terrible, living under his roof with his bitterly upset parents. But once again the message got home to me . . . a cog, dispensable, only another young hopeful from an endless queue.

I did not walk out, although it was in my mind to do so for a brief, traumatic period. I stayed on with a different attitude. I kept to myself a good deal more, kept my mouth shut and watched the professional game reveal all its sides to me.

I wonder if football clubs realize the kind of effect the sacking of a player under those circumstances can have on the rest of their players. Far from teaching any kind of lesson, it just made the youngsters wary, suspicious and puzzled as to the reasoning of the club in which they had placed their entire careers.

Later on I was amazed to see the way Tottenham Hotspur treated Pat Jennings and how Arsenal let down George Armstrong.

Pat served Spurs brilliantly and consistently from the day they bought him from Watford. The big Northern Ireland international goalkeeper repeatedly exhibited his talent, loyalty, sportsmanship and professionalism.

Spurs won League Cup Finals at Wembley, an FA Cup Final and the UEFA Cup with Pat guarding their goal. He virtually kept out Wolves on his own in that 1972 UEFA Cup Final.

Yet when the time came to renew his contract, Spurs refused.

Spurs obviously decided that Pat was over the hill, getting on, past it, on the way down and whatever other charming expression is used to observe that a player is coming to the end of his career.

The business wheels clicked over. Pat's age no doubt came up, as did the pressure coming from Reserves goalkeeper Barry Daines, who naturally enough, wanted to get into the first team.

Pat ended up crossing North London, joining Arsenal for a reported £40,000 fee that made him the bargain buy of the century!

Spurs blundered and suffered for that heartless blunder for seasons afterwards. While they fumbled around trying to solve their goalkeeper problems. Pat helped Arsenal to reach successive FA Cup Finals and continued to excel for his country.

The sad part of it all, however, is that big Pat did not want to leave White Hart Lane in the first place. Not that his feelings mattered a damn. But, although not the type of individual to make public his feelings of disappointment, Pat was hurt by Spurs, hurt by the whole unfeeling system.

So was Geordie Armstrong, one of the most loyal and dedicated pros I ever met.

Geordie served Arsenal through thick and thin, played wherever they put him, ran his heart out as they won glorious triumphs in the 1970s and proved to be one of the stalwarts during the troublesome years of changing management and discontent that followed.

As an example to youngsters, Arsenal had in Armstrong a

priceless asset. With the club from schooldays, he was never any trouble, never commented about club nor team-mates in the newspapers, refused to be drawn into any rows that might damage the club's reputation and believed, unswervingly, that his loyalty would be repaid in some simple fashion.

When Geordie came to the conclusion that his playing career was nearing its end at the top-level, he asked for a transfer in order to secure his future outside the game when his career ended altogether.

But he was still of some use to the club, so they refused. He tried again and this time was promised a problem-free move by Christmas of the season if he stayed on and played while needed. Armstrong did what he was asked. He played his usual 100 per cent game and kept his side of the bargain.

When the time came, he was kicked in the teeth. They wanted a sizeable transfer fee for him.

The whole thing became a bitter saga with Geordie growing more and more disillusioned with the club for whom he believed he had given his all. There were times during the peak of his career that Armstrong could have moved to another club. But he loved Arsenal – genuinely. It was his life.

It was very sad to see him joining Leicester City with bitterness in his heart. It was eventually sorted out, but there was no doubt in Geordie's mind that Arsenal lied to him, let him down and treated him like a piece of movable furniture.

We saw it happen, some players shrugged their shoulders, thinking I don't know what. Would it happen to them some day? Was it worth staying with one club all your career if that is all they think of you in the end?

Geordie ended up with a testimonial match against Barcelona, and came out financially better off. But even that was dodgy. I have heard of players actually losing money because they went ahead and staged testimonial games which, because of the team's poor form at the time or rotten weather, attracted far fewer fans than anticipated.

No. Armstrong, Jennings, Donaldson . . . just three examples of hundreds in a game that has never truly got to grips with the fact that, for all the money talked about and all the glamour and excitement, clubs still treat players like second-class citizens. The businessmen running football dislike players becoming business-like.

I honestly believe they would be much happier if we turned up for training, doffed our caps, shut our mouths and just performed . . . gratefully, of course.

10

Out of Darkness . . .

As Malcolm Macdonald and Alan Hudson boarded the plane for the first stage of their long and lonely journey home in disgrace, I could only envisage yet another season of rows, transfer requests and mediocrity.

There was nothing to indicate that we would reach the semi-final of the Football League Cup and miss Wembley by a goal; nothing to give us reason to believe we would meet Ipswich Town in the 1978 FA Cup Final; not a single pointer to our ultimate qualification to compete in the UEFA Cup.

But then we still had not grasped the full significance of Don Howe's return to Highbury.

In July, the rumours were still flying around concerning the identity of Arsenal's 'new appointment'. And as we were thousands of miles away on the other side of the world and fed up to the back teeth with an exhausting, trouble-torn tour, nothing mattered more than getting home.

Whatever the rights and wrongs of the Macdonald and Hudson case, Arsenal's treatment of their two players was controversial.

They were packed off like two naughty schoolboys to face an army of newspaper, radio and television reporters and cameramen at Heathrow Airport.

Bleary-eyed from non-stop travel, jet-lagged and angry they walked straight into a barrage of questions and flashing bulbs.

It must have surprised even the most experienced media men when they discovered that Macdonald and Hudson were returning alone, without a club representative around to see them through the Heathrow inquisition. As it turned out both players decided to keep their mouths shut, in spite of what they later described as 'determined interviewing attempts'.

Unfortunately, from that moment the situation became something of a saga. The name of Arsenal FC began to appear in all the type of headlines the great old club dislikes.

Both players were put on the transfer list. But then we all witnessed an example of how a club can dispense justice to suit its own ends.

As I've already mentioned, I had seen this unfair method of judgement result in Dave Donaldson being sacked while Brendan Batson was kept on at Highbury. This time the situation concerned two First Division international players. But the end result was the same – preferential treatment for one, not an awful lot for the other.

Malcolm ended up having tea at the home of chairman, Denis Hill-Wood, where the situation was discussed and the breach appeared to be healed. But Huddy? To my knowledge, nobody at the club went to such lengths as to give him the support of a hand extended in friendship.

I can understand this attitude to a point. To lose Malcolm then would have been stupid. His scoring-power was proven and he was an asset. But Huddy had still to show his best form, and I do not think the club was as concerned with sorting out his case.

Next, almost inevitably, came the Sunday newspaper versions of Arsenal's time in Australia. Malcolm chose the *Sunday Mirror* as his medium, and wrote some very harmless drivel about being bought a gin and tonic by the chairman and returning the compliment.

Alan Hudson's version appeared in the *Sunday People* and informed us of very little more of any importance, or indeed relevance. And then, to add a touch of farce to it all, Terry Neill got in on the act. His side of the story appeared in the *News of the World*.

You can only wonder what the youngsters at Highbury must have thought of the senior staff around that time.

But on 9 August, 1977, Arsenal produced a masterstroke . . . they brought Don Howe back to the club, made him chief coach and handed us over to him.

Never in my life have I witnessed such a change in so many players over such a short space of time.

Those of us too young to have worked under him before knew of Howe's reputation as a coach. His work was behind that League and Cup 'double' side. His spell as manager at WBA ended in failure by his standards, but at Leeds United he returned to coaching and their team blossomed.

I have heard it said that it is bad ever to 'go back', to return to the scene of former triumphs. But Howe made nonsense of this theory in a handful of days.

Pat Rice and Peter Simpson had already told us what to expect, but I noticed the immediate impact Howe made for myself. Because, from being discontented and determined to leave my transfer request in front of the board, I suddenly looked forward to every day, wanted to get down to work, wanted to grasp Howe's methods and literally forgot all about my request for a move.

So much so that the matter was never actually resolved. I did not mention the request again and Arsenal just seemed to let the whole thing die a natural death without even discussing it with me.

With Jimmy Rimmer moving to Aston Villa, the arrival of Pat Jennings was a second big boost for the squad inside a week. We knew and respected Pat from our North London 'derby' matches against Spurs. And, to be absolutely honest, thought they were mad letting him leave.

Of all the daft transfers since the Second World War, this has to top the lot. Arsenal's sharpest bit of work in the market and Spurs' biggest boob.

So now we had a very good squad of players and someone with the ability to get the best out of all of us. You could sense the change in everybody.

Players such as myself, Malcolm Macdonald, Alan Hudson, George Armstrong, Trevor Ross . . . we all had an axe to grind with the club. Howe cannot have found his task an easy one when he arrived. And how odd it must have seemed to him when you consider the strong and successful united squad he left behind with Bertie Mee.

So the fact that Howe won over the whole squad in a matter of days speaks volumes for his talent as a man-handler and coach.

And now we had a clear and defined situation. We saw Terry Neill about things such as wages, transfer requests, contracts, etc. And we worked with Don Howe on football and nothing else.

Howe left none of us in any doubt as to what he demanded from us as professionals – loyalty, discipline, hard work and consistently high standards in all that we did.

These demands sound very grand. And I have no doubt that any coach could make them. But getting a whole squad, many members of which were close to leaving the club, to respond to those demands is another matter.

A number of things struck me about Howe from the start. He is not a man who indulges in small-talk. He speaks his mind openly and to your face. He has no favourites, and in his eyes no player is too big to be verbally taken apart if he steps out of line.

Everything at Arsenal stepped up a gear. Everyone became punctual for training. Lateness meant being disciplined and excuses were not invited!

Contrary to popular belief, Howe does not fine players. But then he does not have to. Being on the receiving end of his anger is far worse than having a set amount of money deducted from your wage packet.

Training was harder. Everyone worked harder. With a new coach we all knew that our places had to be won all over again. The lads who had made a few appearances in the first team the previous season were now itching to get into the side on merit and from the start of the season, and this put a healthy and competitive pressure on the rest of us.

Our opening game that season ended in a 1–0 defeat at Ipswich. But nobody was too disappointed because the game was played in a freak rainstorm. It was dreadful and turned the pitch into a pond. I was hauled off by Howe with twenty-five minutes to go and replaced by David Price. My anger at the time was converted, cleverly, by Howe into a fresh approach on my part and a determination to step up my whole game.

Howe's clever psychological approach is described in more detail in the next chapter.

Ritchie Powling scored our winner against Everton the following Tuesday night at Highbury and he earned us a point away to Wolves on Saturday, 27 August, by scoring in a 1–1 draw.

Ritchie was playing better than I had ever seen him play when a tragic knee injury, suffered in our 3–0 home victory over impressive Nottingham Forest, signalled the beginning of a two-year battle with a series of setbacks.

It was terrible to see him fighting away, trying to get fit and suffering repeated disappointments as his injuries kept flaring up. Having to watch a good friend like Ritchie growing more and more depressed as the months slipped by, really brings it home to you how much of a gamble this game is. The threat of injury is ever present.

This is one side of the game I hope I never have to experience. Frankly, I am not sure if I would cope as well as Ritchie Powling coped. He deserves every good opportunity going in the game after what he has endured.

Shortly after Ritchie was injured, George Armstrong turned his back on the club which had been his life and joined former team-mate Frank McLintock at Leicester City.

I believe he was impressed with Howe, as he had always been. But it went deeper than that. Armstrong's battles with Arsenal soured him, hurt him and forced him to behave totally out of character.

What is worse is that things did not work out at Leicester, neither for Frank nor Geordie. Yet they really could have contributed so much if they had stayed with Arsenal.

Meanwhile, Howe recognized the weakness in our style of playing almost solely to Malcolm's strengths. He did not change that as much as develop it. Malcolm was told plainly that he would have to work harder as a team-man and contribute more to overall play.

Howe made Malcolm more aware that he had to come back and mark opponents at corners and free-kicks, vary his approach work and cover more yards off the ball. But even then, Malcolm did not always comply.

112

Bertie Mee – he helped me a lot in the
early days

Bobby Campbell – I owe him a lot,
despite our rows

Don Howe – bringing him back to the
club was a master stroke

Terry Neill – enthusiastic and ambitious, but unpredictable

Arsenal *v.* Sheffield United, 31 January 1976. I scored the only goal in a 1–0 home win which just kept us afloat in 18th position in the League!

Alan Hudson – temperamental but one of the most gifted players of his time

Malcolm Macdonald – his brashness shook the club

Charlie George oozed class, skill and confidence

Alan Ball – a phenomenal character

Team-mates (*left to right*): Trevor Ross, George Armstrong, myself, Alan Ball, Malcolm Macdonald

John Giles – through his leadership and positive example the Republic of Ireland team has been transformed into a force to be reckoned with in international football

Jimmy Greaves – to watch him in action was an education in itself

Johan Cruyff – mastered everything and everyone around him

George Best – without doubt the greatest player in modern football

Manchester United came to Highbury for a League Cup second-round tie and Malcolm scored twice in a 3–2 win, my goal completing the scoreline. Already, we felt sharper, more organized and confident.

By 12 October, as I flew back to Dublin for Ireland's crucial World Cup qualifying match against Bulgaria, we were in the top half of the table, playing well and feeling more united as a squad than at any time in my career.

Bulgaria held us to a 0–0 draw, effectively dumping us out of the World Cup. This came as a bitter blow because we had fancied our chances in a three-nation group and had blown it.

I came back and discovered that Arsenal had bought Mark Heeley from Peterborough. But the transfer news which surprised me most was the sale of Trevor Ross to Everton.

Neill did not fancy Trevor as a player. It was as simple as that. So he sold him and made a very good buy in Alan Sunderland from Wolves, a player who really added something to the team when he settled in.

Alan made his debut against Manchester United at Old Trafford. We turned it on, winning 2–1 in front of a partisan 53,000 crowd with Malcolm and Frank scoring.

Things certainly worked out better for Malcolm than they did for Huddy. Macdonald was quickly taken off the list after his heart-to-heart with Hill-Wood, but Hudson's seemingly endless disagreement with Neill meant that he stayed on the list, out of the team and increasingly irritable.

A thumping punch by Malcolm floored Terry Yorath early in our home game with Coventry on 12 November. He was, of course, sent off. And to make matters worse he was fined £150 for allegedly bringing the game into disrepute after making gestures during the away game at Norwich.

But we were fifth in the table and through to the fourth round of the League Cup after beating Southampton 2–0 at Highbury with a Brady penalty and a goal by Frank Stapleton. Nothing, it seemed, could break the Howe spell.

The only thing casting a bit of a shadow over everything was the continued waste of Hudson's talents. He was as much in the wrong as he thought Arsenal to be. But nevertheless, as we edged closer and closer to the top of the First Division, we knew that a class player like him would be a tremendous asset if in the right frame of mind.

John Matthews scored twice as we slammed five goals past Hull City in the League Cup fourth round on 29 November. All of a sudden we were being tipped as possible bets for the Final – a situation completely new to people such as myself, Frank, Graham Rix, David Price, David O'Leary and John Matthews.

And I became aware of something else – my scoring rate was improving. Admittedly I had taken over the penalty-taker's role from Malcolm, but I was getting into better positions and hitting more shots at goal. This was part of Howe's idea that every member of the team should contribute a certain amount in departments outside of their own.

The Hudson saga deteriorated further when he was suspended for two weeks following remarks made in newspaper articles.

The bad weather turned pitches into skating rinks as the season entered the New Year. We stood in fourth place in the table, tucked in behind Nottingham Forest, the team everybody expected to blow out.

We really began to see the first signs of Wembley on the horizon after holding Manchester City to a fifth round 0–0 draw.

Pat Jennings was superb and we knew that something was with us that had not been there before in previous seasons. It was a remarkable feeling.

I had scored in every round before the City game and wanted to maintain my run. But the replay with City was a difficult match that looked like dragging into extra time and possibly even a second replay.

The 57,748 Highbury crowd hummed with apprehension as City showed just how good a football side they were. It was even, too even for my liking because, clearly, one goal was going to decide who went through to the semi-final.

It was then that Alan Hudson chose to show the world that he had lost none of his enormous talent. He came on as substitute for John Matthews . . . and turned City inside out. It was a great personal triumph for Huddy who deserved every column inch of the paper space his performance received the next day.

More and more he fetched and carried the ball, deep into City's half, giving to feet, supporting, taking the ball back and switching play from wing to wing. Something had to give and in the end it was City's defence.

As Malcolm burst through, Dave Watson brought him down and I tucked the penalty wide of Joe Corrigan to keep up my goal-a-round record.

The FA Cup and League Cup overlap if you reach the League Cup's semi-final so, with one competition dominating our thoughts, we embarked on another, and far bigger one.

The third-round draw took us to Bramall Lane and what on paper looked like a difficult tie against Sheffield United. But on the day they could not live with us.

Going forward, we threw four men at their defence, Malcolm, Frank, Alan and Graham. We were four up at half-time, and how they kept us from scoring ten is beyond me.

Such was the tempo of the side and the confidence running through the whole squad that we no longer even thought in terms of losing. Gone were the rows and the bad atmosphere. I knew that Huddy still wanted to leave. But I also knew that he rated Howe so much that he wanted to play for him.

In the end Huddy compromised. He stayed on the list and turned on the magic for Howe.

Wolves came to Highbury for the fourth round and I still remembered that 3–0 defeat they inflicted on us in Wolverhampton when we last met in the Cup.

We beat them 3–1 in the League at home two weeks earlier. But none of us believed for one moment that Wolves would be so indifferent two weeks in a row. We were right.

Alan Sunderland got great pleasure out of giving us the lead against his old club. But a fine chipped goal by Kenny Hibbitt put them level, and that was the way it looked like staying until big Bob Hazell lost his head in the last minute, threw a punch at Graham Rix and got sent off.

The big black centre-half had subdued Malcolm for eighty-nine minutes. But as he trudged towards the tunnel, over came the ball and Malcolm's head sent it flying past Paul Bradshaw. One chance, one goal! That was the essence of Macdonald.

As we approached the League Cup semi-final with

Liverpool, we felt absolutely sure of ourselves. We knew our strengths and our weaknesses. Don Howe left nothing to chance.

And with the League Championship also there to be contended, I felt as if, at last, I was playing consistently well and within a team capable of living up to the feats of the Arsenal team I saw disintegrate.

11

In Defence of Coaching

The disappointing international results achieved by England for the best part of the last decade led to an increasing number of people blaming coaching and coaches for failures which were really down to a simple shortage of top-class players.

It has become something of a trend, and a handy answer to difficult problems, to lay the blame for most football ills on coaching.

I have heard it said that there is too much coaching in the game, that coaches stifle the natural talents of young players, that the whole business is just a form of compensation for the fact that too many players in the modern game are no more than ordinary when compared with past 'greats'.

The fact is that I disagree with all of these theories, and believe it is time people realized that the majority of this type of generalized opinion is expressed by so-called 'experts' outside football.

The word 'coaching' covers a very wide variety of aspects of the game.

It applies to the instructional side, the work done by a coach with individual players and with a whole squad. It also applies to the psychological approach adopted by the coach – this obviously varies with different coaches – when he is attempting to get to the core of individuals.

And there is always the important day-to-day work which must be done to iron out problems, again of individuals or the team as a whole. These cannot be solved by the players alone. It is almost impossible to overcome certain problems when you are involved.

If, for example, you are conceding goals from set-pieces such as corners or free-kicks, you definitely need somebody on the outside looking in – a man with the knowledge of the game, and the respect of the players, who can assemble you as a group during training and work out why things are not as tight as they should be.

This is almost a matter of routine for players. They know when things are going wrong and appreciate advice and welcome the opportunity to correct individual, or team, weaknesses.

There are, of course, good coaches and not-so-good coaches. From this point of view the whole subject of coaching can be made to appear so complicated and long-winded that players, especially young players, become confused and bored and end up taking very little notice.

But a successful team always has a good coach behind it.

I believe that criticism of coaching in general has been more fierce over the past ten years than ever before. And when you look more closely at the reasons, or possible reasons, for this 'anti' feeling, it does appear to tie in with England's transitional period towards the end of Sir Alf Ramsey's reign and the period when Don Revie was in charge.

Whatever the best club sides achieve during any given era, the standard of football of a country is judged on the performances of the international team.

When Ramsey was in charge he had a handful of world-class players such as Bobby Charlton, Bobby Moore, Gordon Banks and the emerging Alan Ball. No disrespect to the rest of England's World Cup winning squad, but I am now talking about players I can compare with Franz Beckenbauer, Johan Cruyff and Mario Kempes of the more modern era.

From that Ramsey squad came what was later known as the 'Wingless Wonders', a team playing to a 4–3–3 formation who became World Champions in 1966.

Yet Ramsey did have wingers in that England squad – he had Terry Paine, Ian Callaghan and John Connelly. He could have added Peter Thompson and Derek Temple. But after trying a side containing an orthodox winger more than once, he came to the conclusion, and as it proved the correct conclusion, that the best system for the players he had at his disposal was the one he chose.

It was not that Ramsey was obsessed with his new idea, but a more simple fact that he found the best system for the men he had. So by good coaching and intelligent analysis of the whole squad, Ramsey got the best out of his players.

Later, when England's fortunes dipped, we read about Don Revie's dossiers being the cause of the team's apparent confusion and lack of cohesion. Then he was blamed for making too many changes in the England team. Only now and again did someone hit on the real problem. Revie simply did not have enough world-class players at his disposal. Results reflected this, although in many instances he chose formations and selected teams on the same basis as Ramsey had – playing the football which he believed suited his players.

In many ways, it is a bit like the argument about which came first, the chicken or the egg. The word 'coaching' became more and more a word used with critical overtones. People began to accuse the game's tacticians of stifling the natural talents of the nation's young players.

But this is simply not the case. Problems do arise with very young players, schoolboys who become victims of the enthusiasm of their youth team managers and teachers.

When boys are so young that they simply want to play the game without all the technical trimmings thrown in, it is possible to dampen their enthusiasm by making demands on them which, at that age, are totally unnecessary.

I see the real problem as a very human one. The people who run junior teams and school sides usually base their knowledge of the game on the best football they can see, and in this case we are talking about the First Division.

So when they see and hear top players discussing the game, yelling instructions on the pitch, reacting to certain situations in a certain manner, they go back to their youngsters and attempt to get them to play the same way.

It is, of course, a well-intentioned attempt at improving the boys' knowledge and appreciation of the game. But I know that when I was a schoolboy, nobody would have had much success if they had tried to make me mark back, pick up opponents when they got possession and so on. I wanted to enjoy my fantasy world of being whatever star player I had chosen to be on the day.

Under these circumstances it is possible to do some damage to the natural skills of youngsters, filling their heads with the snatches of technical knowledge picked up from textbooks, magazine articles on coaching and games themselves.

But, apart from this aspect of the subject, the game has always thrived on good coaching.

When you consider how football has changed over the decades and how it has developed as a spectacle, it is impossible not to give coaches who have helped to introduce new ideas, formations, set-pieces etc. the credit they deserve.

Do people really believe that the total football of that fine Dutch team in 1974 was achieved by accident or by the automatic grouping of gifted players?

No, the Dutch system of play came about as a result of talented players forming a team which in turn was coached to the extent where the players were giving their best as a unit.

Of course there is always the argument that coaching is the only reason why certain players make the grade as professionals. And that without the efforts of a good coach, certain individuals, not as naturally gifted as others, would never make the grade.

There are two ways of looking at this. I believe that if you look at any of the great sides, from any era, you will discover a definite balance of talents.

How often have you looked at a line-up containing a number of top-class, highly skilled players and wondered how one or two of the other players managed to play in the same team?

What people often forget is that every team requires a good balance, a mixture of strengths to ensure that all the jobs which require doing are done properly. This is where good coaching comes in. You could argue that a team of eleven Cruyffs or Peles would be a soccer ideal. But, of course, it would not.

That is an extreme example of what I mean. But it does not always follow that the best eleven individuals will form the best team. Players have different strengths, and when you take eleven men and combine their strengths in such a way that you have a winning team and an attractive team, then you have achieved a damn good job of coaching.

If you were to sum up the job of a soccer coach, it is to bring out the best in every player at his club. He is the catalyst, the person who sparks the players and gets them playing to the best of their ability, then works at maintaining this level of playing throughout the season.

If a top coach happened to spend some time with schoolboys, the very young boys normally 'coached' by their team manager at park level, he would approach the job in a totally different way from his approach to, say, a First Division squad.

This is an area where most people outside the game seem to have a blind spot. They might expect the coach to bombard kids with the same technical jargon that professional players understand. But without doubt he would encourage the kids to do their own thing at that age and gain confidence.

It is usually the very people who criticize coaching who, if armed with a little knowledge, can make it a very dangerous thing.

I have worked with different coaches and all of them have helped me in some way or other. But it all boils down to the response a man can get from a group of players. If he is unable to stimulate them, fire their imaginations and win their respect, all the technical knowledge in the world will not make that man a good coach.

I worked with Bobby Campbell and Wilf Dixon. They know their jobs well, know what they are talking about. They aim to improve individuals and work very hard at their jobs.

But neither man comes close to achieving the same level of success as Don Howe when it comes to making players respond to him.

John Giles, Dave Sexton and Terry Venables are three more coaches who I would bracket in Howe's class. And that puts them at the very top of the tree.

I never worked with Sexton, nor Venables. But I have seen their teams play, played against them and listened to both men discussing the game. The patterns of approach are familiar. They are top coaches.

One of the most important things in professional football is respect. Players must have it for each other . . . and for the manager and/or coach. Without this you cannot be successful. It breeds confidence and guarantees that problems can be overcome.

Coaching is based on respect – my respect for my coach and his respect for my ability and for me as an individual.

Howe gets through to players that he cares about them and wants to improve them as much as he can. But he demands loyalty, discipline and makes it clear from the start that he has absolutely no favourites.

Working in this atmosphere is enjoyable because you know that you will eventually come out on top. This is all to do with coaching, yet I have not touched on tactics nor on actual play.

In fact it is surprising just how many myths have grown up about coaching in general, nonsense about players being brainwashed, sitting around a blackboard or reading thick dossiers.

But it is the players who need the coach on a day-to-day basis. Not to tell them what line-up they face on Saturday. Not to explain the variations to such-and-such a formation. They need him there because he is the man in charge. He is discipline. He is leadership. He is the person who takes a massive share of the responsibility for what goes on when a team takes the field.

If the coach is a good one, if he is a Howe or a Sexton or a Giles, each player knows that he is watching them and noting their individual form. They know that if something is wrong with their game he will spot it, call them in and work on it.

I am speaking from experience because Howe definitely made me a better player when he came to Arsenal.

There were two things wrong with me around the time he came back to Highbury, and it took him no time at all to spot, and correct, both.

I remember playing reasonably well in the pre-season games, but when we opened our League programme in August 1977, we played at Ipswich in a rainstorm, a real freak downpour that made the pitch a water-trap.

By this time I was recognized as one of the best players at the club. I don't say that immodestly, but I was a regular in the team and playing consistently well enough to hold that status.

122

So the last thing I expected from the new coach was to be pulled off during the opening game of the campaign!

He sent on David Price, leaving me fuming and all the more pleased that I still had a transfer request in front of the board.

But when I complained about the substitution Howe looked straight at me and said: 'I considered it best for the team to take you off and to send on David Price. I am the chief coach and that was my decision. There is nothing more to be said.'

Just when I thought I was really on the way out, Howe shook me up a bit. He probably thought I was drifting too much and needed a reminder of what the game demands from players.

Without my knowing it, my attitude was wrong at that time and the moment he realized that, Howe acted.

I was back in the team for the next game and went on to enjoy my best season at Highbury since the beginning of my career.

Not long after that incident at Ipswich, Howe pulled me to one side and told me bluntly that my concentration was not good enough. He gave me advice, I acted upon it and my game improved.

And the great thing is that I knew that he would keep watching and would pounce on me the moment he thought I was slipping back into a bad habit.

There is no way a player can achieve such things on his own. He needs good advice from a person he respects. That is the essence of good coaching. That's why Arsenal are lucky to have Don Howe.

He is the type of coach who will discuss a particular tactic with his players for ages, then remind them that all the best devised plans in the world can be, and will be, wrecked by one stroke of individual genius.

And when he says that, you know that he has found the simple way of telling you how magical football can be.

Any good coach will admit two things: (a) he cannot coach natural talent into a player who does not have any to begin with; and (b) he cannot coach a player to the point where he can stop a man with natural talent from succeeding.

So when you are in football and you hear top coaches saying 'There is no substitute for skill and flair' you wonder why people jump on band-wagons such as the anti-coaching brigade.

I have come to the conclusion that the majority of critics are convinced that coaching is only concerned with negative aspects of football, and that coaching only concerns defending, shutting down opponents, locking out dangerous forwards.

Nothing could be further from the truth.

Every great team to emerge during the history of the game did so bearing their own hallmark. From the 'third-back' game introduced by Herbert Chapman at Arsenal in the 1930s to the Herrera-style back four plus sweeper as used by Inter Milan in the 1960s. Ramsey's 4–3–3 side, Holland's total football, Liverpool's possession and steam-roller effect and so on.

All the dangerous aspects of successful teams are created through good coaching, introducing new ideas, sometimes only because they happen to suit the players available at the time and arise because those players are there.

Howe has a reputation as a man who concentrates on defence but does not know as much when it comes to forward play. This is nonsense.

He works on the logical basis that if you don't concede a goal you cannot lose. So he gets things working correctly in every department, beginning with the defence.

Howe neglects nothing. That is what makes him top-class.

Sometimes people come away from a boring game complaining that once again a team which has been over-coached has failed to entertain.

In fact is far more likely that the team which bored them stiff did so because it lacked decent coaching!

So to every youngster coming into the game, I say this – accept the fact that you need help with your game. Do not come in with fancy ideas about 'showing those coaches a thing or two'. They will show you lots of things and, if you pay attention and work hard, you will find that coaching will improve you as a player and as a professional.

12

My Part in the Wembley Disaster

Success is relative. If you have won something big in the game and later miss out on a major honour by a narrow margin, you are inclined to consider such a disappointment as a failure. But when you have never won anything at club-level, almost winning something is as close as you have ever been to success.

So it was with our League Cup semi-final against Liverpool. For lads like Pat Jennings, Pat Rice, Alan Hudson and Malcolm Macdonald, the road to Wembley was a familiar one. But for Graham Rix, David Price, Dave O'Leary, Willie Young, Frank Stapleton and myself, the prospect was exciting in a way only someone who has experienced the same feeling can appreciate.

7 February 1978 was the date of the first leg, at Anfield. Despite our good form, the predictions outside our camp were that Liverpool would probably build up a two-goal lead. In fact they should have come to Highbury needing a victory!

With Huddy and I seeing a good deal of the ball, we remained composed and changed ends level at 1–1. Malcolm scored our goal and this must have given him great satisfaction after Tommy Smith's criticisms in the papers.

I still remember Frank Stapleton beating Ray Clemence with a low shot only to see it cleared off the line by a defender. That was the kind of trouble we gave them. Yet Ray Kennedy snatched a winner that we genuinely begrudged them.

Only one game, on our own ground, stood between us and the chance of playing at Wembley. So when Liverpool came to our place on 14 February, we were confident of making up the deficit.

It was that night that I saw everything that is great about Liverpool. Under tremendous pressure, they never panicked and kept on playing their own type of football, holding the ball and biding their time.

Frustration crept into our game because the longer the goal took to score the more Liverpool grew in confidence.

The turning point was all about one breakaway. Malcolm spun on his toes and left the whole Liverpool defence for dead. As Ray Clemence raced out, Malcolm shot . . . and the ball thundered past England's goalkeeper, nicked the far post and came out.

It was a maddening moment because I felt sure that Liverpool's containing game would have collapsed if we had just got that one, equalizing goal.

Naturally we were terribly disappointed afterwards. But the fact that we had come so close to real success compensated for a lot of the let-down. After all those seasons of empty months and failed ambitions, we had proved that we were ready to compete with the best in the land for the top prizes.

Boosted by our League Cup run we attacked the First Division with renewed confidence. And, of course, the FA Cup was suddenly seen as something for which we had almost been rehearsing.

Four days after going out of the League Cup, we played Walsall at Highbury in the fifth round of the FA Cup. And I must say that I thought it all very daft and meaningless the way so many people inside the club, and in the newspapers, kept going on about the pre-war Cup tie in which Walsall beat Arsenal 2–0 during the reign of Herbert Chapman.

I am all for tradition. And I have no doubt that this result was one of the true 'giant-killings' in the competition's history. But to suggest it bore one iota of relevance to our tie was comical.

As we had done at Bramall Lane, we killed the match as a competitive tie inside the first forty-five minutes. Three goals floored Walsall and, although Alan Buckley gave the Midlanders in the 43,736 crowd something to warm their journey home, we scored a fourth to emphasize our superiority. At no stage was there a chance of us going the way Herbert

Chapman's players had gone!

Alan Hudson was now playing very well in midfield and we threatened to move up the First Division table for a late, decisive attack on Nottingham Forest's increasingly impressive lead.

Manchester City were beaten 3–0 at Highbury on 4 March, nudging us up to fourth place. Meanwhile, the draw for the FA Cup quarter-final sent us across the border into Wales for a very difficult tie with Wrexham.

One look at Wrexham's Cup progress was enough to warn us of what lay in store at The Racecourse ground. Although a Third Division side at the time, Wrexham's anticipated attendance was around 25,000. And on their way through from the first round of the competition they won 2–0 away to Preston North End, drew 4–4 away to Bristol City and won the replay 3–0 then drew 2–2 at St James Park, Newcastle and romped the replay 4–1.

So, on 11 March we faced a side brimming with confidence, close to winning promotion to the Second Division and backed by a fanatical Welsh crowd. But it is on occasions such as these that players really appreciate the support they receive from the hard core of travelling fans who show up no matter what corner of the globe you play.

The Arsenal supporters did us proud at Wrexham and Malcolm's first-half goal silenced the singing in the valleys temporarily. The second half was a fast and furious affair that brought four goals – one of them scored by Alan Sunderland and one by big Willie Young, his third, and most valuable, goal of the season.

Wrexham gave us a difficult time. It was the type of Cup tie most First Division teams would have been delighted to draw. But the fact that we marched into our second semi-final of the season at the first attempt only added to the confidence running right through the team.

Then the news filtered through as we washed and changed . . . West Bromwich had beaten Forest 2–0, little Orient held Middlesbrough to a 0–0 draw at Ayresome Park and Ipswich had trounced Millwall 6–1 at The Den.

Arsenal woke up on Sunday, 12 March, and found themselves FA Cup favourites! This was cemented by the semi-final draw which paired Albion with Ipswich, ironically to be played at Highbury, and us with the winners of Orient *v* 'Boro.

To be honest, we expected 'Boro to sneak it by, perhaps, one goal. But Orient excelled themselves, winning the replay 2–1, adding another scalp to those of Chelsea and Norwich whom they knocked out in earlier rounds, both away from home.

Doubtless the fans were delighted that we had drawn a Second Division club in the semis. And while our confidence lifted us above everything at that time, there is always the nagging doubt when it comes to playing 'one-off' games against teams from lower divisions . . . especially in the FA Cup.

Sometimes it is better to face another First Division club – a team of players familiar to you, whose style of play will not take you by surprise and whom you may have already played twice in League matches that season.

Through all the mounting excitement, one man remained absolutely calm and analytical – Don Howe. It made no difference to him whether we played Orient or Liverpool. He brought us down to earth and prepared the team for the forthcoming League games, pointing out that we were still in that particular hunt, and that the League represents the bread and butter of all players.

Winning the Cup guarantees entry into Europe via the Cup Winners' Cup. But we knew that a place in the top four would qualify us for a place in the UEFA Cup no matter what happened in the FA Cup.

Bristol City were beaten 4–1 at Highbury on 18 March. We drew 1–1 at Birmingham, hammered WBA 4–0 at our place, Malcolm scoring a hat-trick, drew 0–0 away with Chelsea. Arsenal moved into third place and it seemed as if we had peaked at just the right time.

The young players undoubtedly gained invaluable experience from the League Cup run – coping with pressure as the competition thinned out to the last four, handling the media and maintaining a consistency in the League.

The forwards were certainly clicking and it was the first sign of things going wrong when Alan Sunderland, who had scored seven priceless goals since his arrival from Wolves, broke a bone in a leg during the 4–0 win over Albion.

Graham Rix came back into the team and replaced Alan on the wing – a move which meant the team kept up its momentum as if nothing had happened.

Our last League game before the semi-final was against Manchester United, at Highbury. They were in mid-table and slipping back into top gear after a lean spell so we were provided with an ideal test.

We beat them, 3–1, Malcolm (2) and I scoring, and at last got down to our plans to deal with Orient at Stamford Bridge.

Ireland beat Turkey 4–2 in a friendly international in Dublin on the Wednesday night, 5 April, and I felt a little bit strange not being there, but considered the result a good omen for the Irish lads in the team.

Orient were operating a defensive but effective system which saw Glen Roeder playing as a spare man behind, and often well behind, a back four which included two big central defenders, Phil Hoadley and Nigel Gray. Up front they relied a lot on the speedy breaks of Peter Kitchen, feeding off centre-forward Joe Mayo.

This 'soak up pressure and counter-punch' style of play caught Norwich, Chelsea and 'Boro on the hop. But Don Howe had the whole system analysed down to the last detail. We went into that game feeling more confident than I imagine any semi-finalists have ever felt.

On the day, we were simply too good for Orient. Perhaps one or two of them froze. But Howe's tactics worked a treat. We attacked them from very wide positions, Malcolm and Frank veering away from the middle, leaving Orient's choking group of defenders somewhat bemused.

Naturally, this type of attack pulled their defence wider and before very long Orient realized that things were building up against them at an alarming pace.

Malcolm proved the match winner. His first goal was viciously deflected. In fact a lot of people claimed his shot would have struck the corner flag had it not cannoned off a defender's back and wide of John Jackson. But his second goal, also deflected, gave Jackson little chance, and when Graham

Rix made it 3–0 in the second half, there came a time when it looked as if we might run up the biggest semi-final margin of victory for many years.

The atmosphere afterwards was fantastic. Some of us were lost for words. We were going to Wembley. A season that had begun in such sour circumstances was turning into the greatest of my career.

And the two players who came so close to being chopped from the club before a ball had been kicked – Macdonald and Hudson – were playing a big part in the success.

Usually, players who look back on FA Cup Finals only remember their win in terms of the excitement and celebrations after the match. Many players say that the actual day flies by too quickly for them to let the whole occasion sink in.

In our case, all the happiness and celebrating came after the semi-final. Because what happened from there on in became a nightmare.

My last home game of the season was against Newcastle in which I scored my thirteenth goal of the season in a 2–1 win. This represented the biggest total of goals scored by me in one season . . . and it was certainly a case of unlucky thirteen!

We kept chipping away at the top two clubs and our 3–1 win away to Leeds gave the press fresh ammunition to fire at Bobby Robson's Ipswich Town whose 3–1 semi-final victory over West Bromwich Albion upset most predictions and seemed to increase our standing as favourites.

Disaster struck me on 25 April. We lost a close game, 1–0 at Liverpool. But I was carried off with a badly injured right ankle – a knock destined to keep me awake for successive nights as the awful thought of missing the Final kept hitting me.

I missed our last League game of the season in which a Frank Stapleton goal ensured two points and left us a very respectable fourth in the table. At last we knew that we had qualified for a place in Europe, something to balance the growing anxiety in the camp.

Ipswich, it seemed, were the walking wounded. Robson managed to give the press a story a day about the injuries threatening to sideline Kevin Beattie, Allan Hunter and just about every player on his staff.

Added to the fact that we were favourites, this increased the pressure on us – definitely one point up for Robson who did a good public relations job for his team.

But the truth was that Highbury, and not Portman Road, was the casualty ward.

My ankle was painful, swollen and stubbornly refusing to improve. Alan Sunderland was battling to be ready for the Final but clearly lacked match fitness. Pat Rice was carrying an ankle injury that was worse than anybody outside the club realized. And Malcolm Macdonald was doing his best to hide the fact that his right knee was giving him increasing trouble.

What nobody outside the club knew was that some of us approached Wembley with genuine fear in our hearts.

I certainly did. And Alan Sunderland admitted to me afterwards that he had felt the same. Pat's experience kept him calm – it was his third FA Cup Final, and Malcolm was going back to Wembley for his third Final looking for his first winners medal. But nevertheless they both must have felt some sense of worry.

No injured player can avoid the feeling of nagging doubt. He may be able to fool everyone else. But he cannot fool himself. And if he knows that he is less than 100 per cent fit, his game suffers. To any lad coming into the game I give the following advice. Never gamble with an injury. If you are not fit, do not play. You risk worsening the injury and letting down your team-mates.

As the days flew by and the date for the naming of the team approached I felt a cold sensation in the pit of my stomach. I wanted to play more than anything I had ever wanted in my life. And I knew that both Terry Neill and Don Howe wanted me to be fit. In the end I declared myself fit to play. But it was the biggest single mistake I have ever made.

The team sheet was pinned up for all to see on Thursday, 4 May. My name was on it. Graham Rix's was not.

I will never forget the look on his face when he realized that he was not playing. He had been involved all the way in our Cup run and was certainly in a position to claim something that four of us on that team sheet could not – that he was 100 per cent fit. As I saw Graham trying to conceal his bitter disappointment I knew that I had made a mistake. To make matters worse he is one of my best mates and I still feel a sense of guilt when I look back at that traumatic week.

You have to take into consideration the fact that reaching a Cup Final is such a special thing. And for the majority of players something that happens either once in a lifetime or never at all.

There are men in the game today – like Don Howe, George Best and Coventry's Gordon Milne – who never played in an FA Cup Final.

I was twenty-two, experiencing my first taste of success in a season during which I had already seen a chance of playing at Wembley snatched away at the last minute by Liverpool.

I don't think many teams went through what a lot of the Arsenal lads suffered before the Final. We sat in the dressing-room, geeing each other up and approaching it with just the right attitude as a team.

But from my own point of view I knew deep down that I could not play to my fullest capacity. Looking back, Malcolm must have gone through the same kind of hell.

His knee had reached the stage where he had to grab his instep with his hand and pull his right leg up behind him in order to flex the knee joint and keep it from getting stiff.

We knew their style of play – the long, deep ball that is aimed to put you under immediate pressure, the strong running of Brian Talbot and John Wark in midfield, the danger posed by Clive Woods' tantilizing runs on the left wing, the sharpness and close-control of Paul Mariner, all backed up by the strong and experienced defensive partnership of Kevin Beattie and Allan Hunter at the heart of their defence.

Ironically it was the enormous contributions of two lesser-known players which resulted in Ipswich winning the FA Cup for the first time in their history.

One of our great strengths lay on the left-side of the pitch. I am sure Ipswich anticipated trouble from the combination of myself, Sammy Nelson and Malcolm Macdonald. So Bobby Robson obviously planned to shut off that avenue of attack, not realizing just how limited my contribution was going to be anyway.

He played David Geddis wide on their right, a ploy which kept Sammy busy for most of the match. And it was to be Geddis who set up the eventual winner for Roger Osborne.

My injury plus Sammy's preoccupation with Geddis prevented us from operating the triangular movements Huddy and I worked with Sammy on that side of the pitch.

Yet we made a bright enough start and Dave O'Leary almost gave us an early lead with a shot that flew just wide. But Mariner ran at our defence with venom and, after shooting wide, hit the bar with a tremendous drive.

This gave Ipswich the lift they needed to put their plans into play. Talbot ran long and hard, covering acres of pitch; Woods gave Pat Rice an armful of problems down the left wing and we could not get Frank and Malcolm functioning sharply enough to lose Hunter and Beattie.

I became aware of my ankle and of the obvious fact that Alan Sunderland was not match-fit. He lacked his usual sharpness and pace on the right side of our attack, while Malcolm had begun pulling at that instep to unlock his knee.

For all the encouragement and good advice Terry Neill and Don Howe gave us at half-time, Ipswich seemed to have the bit firmly between their teeth. John Wark twice hit the woodwork and Pat Jennings made a marvellous save from a George Burley header.

But in the end it was too much for my ankle. And as I limped off, feeling worse than at any time in my life, I was reminded that the man replacing me, Graham Rix, should have been out there in the first place.

Osborne's winner some thirteen minutes from time was not a real shock. We were up against it in a match which most people predicted we would dominate. I accept that excuses are a waste of time, but the injury situation cannot be ignored. Arsenal played that game with four players less than 100 per cent fit, and that is a handicap no team can overcome.

Afterwards I wanted to get away from everybody. I cried my eyes out and simply could not stop. I really believed that I had just had my one and only Cup Final chance. And those kind people who tried to cheer me up by saying that we would be back the following year only made me feel worse.

It is a lovely sentiment, but very few teams have managed to reach successive Cup Finals in the history of the competition. And the way I felt that evening there was no way I could see us getting a second chance.

On that one occasion I had to drown my sorrows, and was in bed by 9.00 p.m.

A few days later Malcolm entered hospital for the first of a series of operations that were eventually to bring about the end of his career. He would never play at Wembley again. In fact his career stretched only as far as a handful of games the next season, a short spell in Sweden, then enforced retirement at twenty-nine.

Don Howe did a great morale job on the squad. He pointed out how far we had come so quickly and also how young the majority of the team was. All solid, sensible observations which, when they sank in and the disappointment slowly faded, helped us to pick up the pieces and look at the season in a new light.

I put it all behind me by joining the Irish squad for a friendly game in Oslo. We drew 0–0 with Norway on 21 May, but my ankle was still painful and I was replaced during the game by Ashley Grimes.

Three days later Ireland, without me, went 3–1 up against Denmark in Copenhagen in their first 1980 European Championship qualifying tie. Sadly, the Danes forced a 3–3 draw, the first of the priceless points we dropped in a group eventually won by England.

I looked back over the season while nursing that ankle injury. It ruined my Cup Final dream, forced me to miss my country's first competitive international of the European Championship and led me to make a dreadful error of judgement.

But it was still a successful season, one in which I learned a lot of very important things about the game, myself and my values in life.

It was the season when one man, Don Howe, rescued a sinking ship single-handed, a season which saw the new, young Arsenal emerging from the ashes of great predecessors, and a season in which I tasted the real sweetness of success followed by the awful sourness of failure.

Only when you have experienced failure can you truly appreciate success. That is what they say, and as the coming months were to prove, they never said a truer word!

13

The Essence of Greatness

George Best, Jimmy Greaves, Johan Cruyff, Bobby Moore . . .
the names roll off your tongue with an ease tinged with respect.
These are the men I consider to be, or who have been, professional footballers 'plus'. The 'plus' is all about class, and these
men oozed it.

It seems the thing to do in these books is to name your world
eleven or select your team from the best players in the game's
history. I am not going to comply.

I want to talk about superstars, those very special players
who capture the imagination, set fire to a crowd and a team,
and who manage to display their talent consistently, at the
highest levels.

Like everyone else, I have my favourites. I will name them.
But I will also attempt to analyse them as individuals, list their
strengths and explain why I consider them to be the best in the
game's long catalogue of great players.

I have not been in the professional game that long. But I
have read the same books every football-loving kid has read,
seen the same great televised matches, followed the World
Cups with fervent interest and taken every opportunity to see
the players whom I consider to be at the top of the profession.

Bearing all this in mind, I have no hesitation in naming
George Best as the greatest player in modern football.

No doubt this devastating Ulsterman had weaknesses. But
they were microscopic when compared with his strengths. I
talk in the past tense because I am referring to the Manchester
United Best, the frail-looking teenager who unleashed a talent
of such enormity that he attracted a whole new dimension of

publicity, adulation and criticism, and ultimately buckled under the pressures.

His later career with Fulham, various clubs in the USA and Scottish League side Hibernian proved the man's magnetism. Because for all his errors of judgement with regard to his own career, he is special and continues to hold a very special place in the hearts of those people who love great ability and skill.

I look at Best and think: 'God, this man can carry on playing good football as long as he lives.' Why? Because his brain can continue even when his body flags. As his natural speed diminishes, so Best will restrict his physical output, pacing himself and compensating more and more with his unique level of skill, vision and perception.

The Best of United's sixties era was a phenomenon. And oddly enough, he often failed to get the credit he deserved for attributes in addition to the pace, skill and scoring talents for which he was widely known.

Best's courage deserves more praise than it received over the years. Imagine how the average player felt – indeed still feels on occasions – when faced with the brooding, unpredictable Best. Such was the fear that he struck into players' hearts that he took more stick in one game than most players take in a month.

His heading could not be faulted, his work-rate was tremendous and his tackling superbly timed and very effective.

I bow to the greatness of Pele, di Stefano, Puskas and the like. But for me George Best was the most complete player of all.

You can only wonder what he might have achieved under different circumstances. What so many people tend to forget is that the combination of being who he was and playing for a club like United created a publicity monster. It nicked pieces out of his life until he could stand no more.

I agree that George made mistakes. But the nature of them is not for me to say. The fact that he did not carry on longer at the very top is proof enough that something went terribly wrong in his life.

Maybe his talent was too great. All the same, even people who knew nothing about football were attracted to Best by the nature of his gift, a sure sign of greatness.

They, as well as the terrace fanatics, could see that Best's talent on the field was both instinctive and calculated. He played the way nature intended, but he was always aware of things going on around him, sensing openings before they appeared, probing for and finding weaknesses in the strongest defences and posing continual problems simply because he could do things with a ball that most players only dream of doing.

Ironically, many young players – myself included – owe Best a debt of which I doubt if he is even aware.

The modern game is heavily involved in big finance, and players are constantly in the limelight. And while every young-ster worth his salt wants to make it to the top, he does so know-ing that when he gets there he will have to learn to live with certain pressures and headaches.

There are also many dangers at this level. Hangers-on are a good example, the back-slapping well-wishers who do you absolutely no good at all by telling you that the rubbish match you have just played was everyone else's fault but yours.

I believe that Best's whole life, from the greatness of youth to the bitter disappointments of his mid-career and the repeated attempts at making up for lost years in his thirties, stands out like a beacon for every youngster coming into the game.

All the things that can happen to a gifted young man appeared to happen to Best. Newspaper stories he could have done without, pictures snapped with pretty girls at various pubs and clubs, marriage rumours, drinking confessions, rows, walk-outs, non-appearances, tantrums and so on.

He fell prey to a lot of the dangers. And because of his fame and talent, his departure from the big-time so early was not only a tragic waste but also a constant red light to people like me, warning me what can happen, what will happen, and how to come to terms with success, fame and comparative fortune.

The first time I met George Best he completely turned my childhood upside down with a few quietly-spoken words.

I attended a PFA Awards Dinner early in my career, at a time when I was in the running but did not win the title. I met George who, through all the fuss and bother, remained the same basic character – quiet, a bit shy and unable to hide the fact that he was often lonely in crowded rooms.

He was genuine and friendly in conversation as we chatted about the game in general. But even as I was talking I recalled my countless games on many a Dublin pitch during which I decided to be George Best for ninety minutes. He was one individual who appealed to me more than any other, the player who excited me most and whom I most wanted to emulate.

So you could have removed my chair and left me floating when he casually revealed that he had voted for me and hoped I would win the award!

After all those years of nearly idolizing him, here was Best voting for me as a potential Players' Player.

Football must produce hundreds of players every season, new faces, fresh hopes, varied talents . . . but how many are still remembered by the fans in their own playing careers, let alone after they retire? It is the handful who come into the George Best calibre who merit the title 'great'.

So what is it, apart from the obvious, visible ability of the individual, that makes a player great?

Well perhaps 25 November 1979 provides me with a good example. On that Saturday, Manchester United beat Norwich 5–0 to establish top-spot in the First Division, Nottingham Forest lost their third consecutive League match, Brian Clough threatened that all was not so hot at the City ground and the All Blacks beat England 10–9 at Twickenham.

But what made the majority of back-page Sunday newspaper headlines? The Scottish League debut of thirty-three-year-old George Best for virtually-doomed-to-relegation Hibernian.

A crowd of more than 13,000 saw St Mirren beat visiting Hibs 2–1 – over double the club's average Premier Division attendance, and Best gave them value for cash with a last-minute goal thrown in for good measure.

The reports of the game that filtered south all contained the one consistent factor – that every time Best got the ball, the crowd buzzed with anticipation. And that, more than anything else, is the key to a great player.

The man who can bring a whole stadium of fans to their toes every time the ball goes near him is the man with the magician's touch.

Watch out for it next time you are at a match, and note how many players do not spark this reaction from the supporters.

Denis Law created this atmosphere, so did Jimmy Greaves, Pele, the men with the gift for producing the unexpected. Even on their off days they created a very special tingle in those who watched them. Because people sensed that they were watching something out of the ordinary.

If Best was the greatest player I ever saw then Greaves was the greatest goal-scorer. For as long as I am fortunate enough to play professional football I will never be able to achieve the standard of coolness in the box that Greaves made his trade-mark.

Summing him up is difficult because he was more than just a goal-scorer, contrary to popular opinion. The skill of Greaves and his ability to read situations so early was enough to make your hair stand on end, especially if you happened to be the man sentenced to the job of marking him.

Greaves's timing was immaculate. And this was how he beat so many offside traps to score remarkable solo goals for Chelsea, Milan, Spurs, West Ham and England. To watch him in action was an education in itself. Often he would deliberately take up a position in the box which, on the face of it, looked the wrong place to stand. Yet the number of times he got possession inside the penalty area and whipped the ball cleanly past the goalkeeper is sufficient proof that he knew exactly what he was doing, and why.

His great strength was his ability to stay absolutely cool in the one part of the pitch where the temperature is usually at boiling point – inside the box.

Even now, after more than five years of First Division football, international matches and Cup Finals, I am as likely as the next player to hurry chances when I get them. The killer instinct of the natural goal-scorer is something inside the man. It is not something you can acquire by 'keeping at it'.

I have belted in some good goals from a distance. But I have also raced on to good chances and shot too soon from inside the area. Greaves appeared to make time when in fact he had none. It was as if he saw nobody else inside the area, nobody except the goalkeeper.

And his style of finishing, the beautifully-placed strike, clean and efficient with the minimum of back-lift, gave neither goalkeeper nor marker much advance warning. He could explode a twenty-yard shot, especially with his left foot, in mid-stride with hardly a trace of back-lift.

I remember playing against Greaves in Pat Jennings's testimonial at White Hart Lane. Unlike a lot of these games, our meetings with Spurs were always serious and competitive. Neither players nor fans would have it any other way.

The game finished 2–2, and needless to say Greaves scored both Spurs goals. I was tremendously impressed by him, the way he sniffed out the openings, the way he paced himself and especially the way he put the ball in the net.

Hardly surprising that, even on that night, years after Greaves's retirement from League football, he created that buzz every time he homed in on goal . . . and gave First Division defenders, some of them nearly half his age, moments of genuine anxiety.

When Johan Cruyff took over the mantle as the best player in the world, he immediately realized that he was only sitting up there waiting to be shot down. He knew that every opponent would try extra hard to make an impression, like the old cowboy story of the weary gunfighter who gets to the stage of being afraid to stand with his back to anybody, anywhere, in case some fame-hunting youngster shoots him in the back.

Cruyff's gifts enabled him to play virtually anywhere. He scored goals as a striker for Dutch side Ajax and for Holland. Later he engineered their European Cup triumphs before signing for Barcelona where he became a kind of midfield general, dictating the pace of games and the direction of most passes.

English fans saw him wreck their international team at Wembley when two Jan Peters goals gave Holland a 2–0 victory. The scoreline was irrelevant. It was the comprehensive way in which Cruyff mastered everything and everybody around him.

He made his side tick and tore England asunder with remarkable vision, passing, running off the ball and creativity.

I had first-hand experience of just how great a player he is when Barcelona came to Highbury for George Armstrong's testimonial match.

It was a very competitive affair and a game which we all knew involved prestige and reputations. I was doing my best to make an impact on the night while Cruyff and Co. seemed to be playing well within themselves without really giving us much trouble.

But then we had the audacity to take the lead . . . and that was the end of that. Cruyff took over, almost as if he physically changed gear, and he took us apart. I remember his unbelievable shooting, front-foot passing and sheer ball-skills as Barcelona beat us 3–1.

I also became aware of the Arsenal supporters applauding him more and more, simply because his skills rose above the differences between shirt colours and team names. His was such a special talent that he entertained and excited everyone in the ground.

After the game I saw him in the players' lounge and to my surprise he came over to speak to me. I was still new to the big-time and, to be honest, I was chuffed that Cruyff even recognized me in my off-field clothes.

He took me to one side and said: 'You played very well tonight. If you keep playing like that, things will go very well for you in the future. Keep playing the way you played against us.'

Those few words gave me such a thrill that I could not get them out of my head for days. It is moments such as that one that stay with a player all through his career.

There are other ways of recognizing a great player apart from the way he makes a crowd sparkle.

Bobby Moore was a world class player and I believe that if Ron Greenwood had a Moore in his mid-twenties as he builds for the 1982 World Cup, then England would go all the way in Spain and become a true world power.

Players of the Moore mould are few and far between. He was one of the main reasons why England won the World Cup in 1966, along with Gordon Banks and Bobby Charlton.

Moore's greatest quality was the way in which he made everything he did on the field look so simple and unhurried. He always had time, always had options and rarely lost possession through bad passing.

Although never a fast player, his reading of the game, his positional sense, his ability to lead through example and his cool, calculating brain gave Moore the weapons of greatness. And how well he carried them and used them.

I believe that he made the players alongside him look twice as good as they really were, especially during his West Ham career.

He covered for people's mistakes, tidied up after their blunders and played the game at his pace, maintaining possession until just the right moment and never booting the ball clear for the sake of safety.

It is ironic that it was not until Franz Beckenbauer came on the scene that people began to realize exactly what Moore could do. He was playing that same type of game for years before Beckenbauer was moved back into defence, and it was strange how the West German player, great player though he was at his peak, received all the acclaim while Moore plugged away in the Football League.

Beckenbauer's style must have had a lot to do with it. He possessed a great gift for deceiving opponents as to his intentions. The 'Kaiser', as he became known, always played with a back as straight as an RSM's.

You could hardly tell when he was going to pass the ball because his head did not appear to move downwards. He had so much control over the ball that he seemed to be looking up all the time and simply passed the ball when he saw the correct situation developing. He knew where the ball was and his touch was firm and sure.

The great danger of Beckenbauer was his ability to break out from behind his own defence and attack the middle of the field with the ball. Coming through as sweeper he was usually free until someone took it upon himself to challenge.

Creating this extra man caused havoc in many games, and Beckenbauer was also confident enough to sweep through the lot and complete his run with a devastating scoring shot.

Moore was neither as fast nor as attack-minded. But his positional sense was out of this world and he, too, spotted the correct moments to leave his defensive duties and carry the ball upfield, although rarely as far nor as frequently as the great West German international.

It is not my intention to list every great player I have seen or played alongside. But I cannot wrap up this subject without mentioning two soccer 'brains', Alan Ball and John Giles.

Both play in midfield, both are leaders, yet their game is basically different. Ball excels at the short game, the give and run, give and run prompting allied with a fanatical will to win and absolutely no patience with people whom he considers cannot play.

Giles was the man who made Leeds tick. They gave him the ball and he decided the speed of the game, he called the moves by virtue of the fact that he held the ball more than anybody else and he could open out a game with a pin-sharp forty-yard ball to a team-mate's feet.

More than anything else, both players operated on their brains. They worked things like mini-computers, even as a game was going on.

Both had a big influence on my career, for which I am openly grateful. But it is not for that reason that I include them in this chapter, more for the fact that few players achieve world-class status. Ball and Giles did. I played with both and have seen their talents first-hand.

And to be absolutely honest, whenever I see either of them in action, I feel a certain buzz of excitement when they get the ball. . . .

14

Stepping into Europe

When something hurts like hell and somebody tells you that the pain is in your imagination you feel inclined to argue. That was the situation I was in as season 1978–79 approached.

My ankle injury kept me more or less inactive during the summer. But even then I immediately feared the worst the moment I did put it to the test. The trouble lay in the ligaments. And I did not feel at all confident about their repair.

After only one friendly game I decided to act quickly. I was really afraid that the injury would keep me out of the opening games of the season. Fred Street helped me to see a specialist who promptly told me that the ankle was healed!

No matter what I said, the man insisted that the only trouble lay in my mind. I was, he said, afraid of putting the ankle under real pressure in case it broke down again.

I doubted his opinion but took his advice . . . and to my amazement discovered that his words were 100 per cent correct. I put the ankle through a few tough tackles and did not feel a twinge.

Perhaps the disappointments of the previous season contributed to my anxiety, but I discovered then just how easy it is to be mistaken about an injury, and how much we can fall victims to our own worst fears.

The all-clear to play brought all that had gone before into sharp focus. Gone was the ache which had stayed with me for ages after the Cup Final. In its place I felt a sense of achievement. We had experienced our first taste of success. And although we had nothing to show for it after two tremendous Cup runs, we did qualify for Europe. And that most certainly is success.

Despite the fact that we pushed Nottingham Forest all the way up to the Cup Final and finished fourth in the First Division in 1977–78, we knew deep down that our squad was not strong enough to win the League Championship.

Not that we adopted a defeatist attitude. Far from it. We were simply being realistic and assessing the whole season on the presumption that the other squads lived up to their full potential and that they avoided serious injury problems. After that, of course, the actual playing of every game brings the unexpected in one way or another.

When we looked at the season during late July and early August, we discussed our UEFA Cup entry in great detail and looked to the two domestic Cups to bring us another action-packed campaign. Above all else, we knew, without actually making an issue of it, that the team had overcome the bad days for good. A new era was actually unfolding and I, for one, wanted to be aware of the experience while it was happening.

It was about this time that I suddenly became aware of my position in the club. I was, despite being twenty-two, one of the longest-serving players in the squad and also one of the most experienced in League football appearances. This led to me becoming looked upon by some of the younger lads as a 'senior'. I must have rated as one of the game's youngest seniors of all time.

Gone were the men of matches totalling in the hundreds and medals in fours and fives. I had to turn and face the rest of the players and accept my share of the responsibility for ensuring that the team ticked over, held together and kept steadily improving.

This was a weird feeling at first. But I also discovered that I enjoyed the responsibility and the fact that I was receiving the respect of my fellow pros. When it comes to the crunch, nothing matters more than this form of respect. If the press hammer you and the fans give you unmerciful abuse, it becomes partly bearable as long as your professional colleagues retain their respect for you and support you publicly.

Paul Barron arrived from Plymouth for around £70,000 as Reserve goalkeeper to Pat Jennings; John Devine, another

146

Dubliner, emerged from the Reserves as a potential First Division full-back; Steve Gatting pushed his claim for a first-team place; Steve Walford came across North London from Spurs to add to the new, young Arsenal; Mark Heeley made good progress in the Football Combination side; Brian McDermott proved that he was close to making the grade at the top level – all young players, full of ambition and fire.

Add to those David Price, David O'Leary, Frank Stapleton and Graham Rix and you can see how I managed to become a senior during that short summer break.

All these players, however, were working hard, as indeed I was, to establish themselves fully. Perhaps I was established in so far as my experience went, but you can take nothing for granted in professional football. And at twenty-two you know that anything can happen.

The youth of the squad was a good thing from the point of view of the future. But as the season opened I believed that we were thin on the ground when it came to experienced First Division players. You only needed two injuries to first-team regulars and the side became slightly top-heavy with youngsters.

That is why the transfer of John Matthews to Sheffield United really surprised me. John did not request a move. I assume United made an offer and Arsenal informed John and gave him the option. But at that time I felt it would have been to the squad's advantage to encourage John to stay.

This feeling grew stronger when Alan Hudson's worsening personality battle with Terry Neill led to his transfer to Seattle Sounders for a reported £100,000. A lot of things have been written and said about Huddy – that he was difficult to manage, inconsistent and, basically, trouble.

There is no denying that his track record was dotted with rows and headlines that he could have done without. And I accept that he is a complex character and a man that I, for one, found it very difficult always to understand, despite knowing him well.

But neither can anyone deny that he is a class footballer, a midfield player of great skill and vision. When he played well for Arsenal he often touched great heights and was a real asset

147

to the side. Unfortunately, his stay at Highbury was a series of highs and lows.

In fact the Cup Final against Ipswich, in which he began well but faded as we failed to compensate for our knocks, was to be his final game for Arsenal's first team. Yet he did not move to Seattle until the October, by which time we had played ten First Division games and been knocked out of the League Cup. That is some indication of the arguments that went on behind the scenes before he got the move he wanted.

I believe Alan felt that the FA Cup was the one thing he could have offered Arsenal as vindication of their decision to buy him, as proof to his critics that they were wrong. But when that Final was lost it only strengthened his resolve to make the break. Perhaps he really felt that it was not to be, that he did not fit into the scene. All I know is that it was another loss to our squad.

Even as he scored his first goal of the season at Maine Road against Manchester City on 22 August, Malcolm Macdonald's knee was deteriorating. Not the right knee, from which they removed a cartilage during the close season, but the left knee – a legacy of an old injury sustained during his Newcastle United days.

I was more aware of injuries then that at any time in my career. I had made the wrong decision concerning the Cup Final then spent the summer worrying if my ankle was going to develop into something serious and long-term. I sensed the fact that Malcolm was carrying the injury on to the field and trying to hide the fact.

He played in the opening match of the season when we drew 2–2 at home with Leeds United. But some of the speed was gone, the reactions also. He was trying, but definitely hindered.

It was a great start for me because I scored both our goals, one from a penalty, but it was also a home point dropped, and it does not matter whether you drop a point in the first game or the last, the value is the same. And it can be just as costly.

Malcolm scored our goal in that 1–1 draw away to City, but the beginning of the end for him was our League Cup, second round tie away to Rotherham United on 29 August.

In all honesty you can take nothing away from Rotherham on a night when they outplayed us fair and square to win 3–1. We were bitterly disappointed because we considered ourselves nicely set up for another good League Cup run after gaining such great experience the previous season.

But on one August night in Yorkshire one whole part of our season was swept into the dust. And I believe that Malcolm was partly responsible.

I have every sympathy for a man wanting to do his best, wanting to keep going. But he was not fit in any of those first three games and it showed. He carried that leg against Rotherham and probably made it worse after taking a heavy challenge in the second half.

We trailed 2–1 at half-time, although Frank Stapleton opened the scoring. But frankly we were always second to Rotherham, especially with only half a strike force.

I was so upset about this that I went to see Terry Neill after the game and told him that I thought Malcolm should not be playing, that it was not doing him any good and certainly was not benefiting the team.

Neill told me that he was manager and that he would make the decisions as to who did and did not play. I don't argue with the strength of the man's case. Just the logic of the whole stupid situation.

So, after only three appearances, a man who had scored no less than forty-one League goals in eighty-one appearances for Arsenal entered hospital for the second time in four months. This time his career was finished. He made a fight of it, even managing to appear, and score, in our last League match of the season – a 1–1 draw at Chelsea. After that he tried a slow, steady climb back to fitness by playing in Sweden during the summer. But it was too much for a damaged joint.

This was the first blow to the squad. And it adds weight to my case for fearing the worst when Matthews and Hudson were also gone by October.

Either side of Huddy's departure I played in two very important games for Ireland, the historical 0–0 draw against the North, played in Dublin, and my second crack at the highly rated English side, which also ended all-square at 1–1 in Dublin.

A few newspapers said that we had not progressed at all since our draw at Wembley. But they were totally wrong. The Wembley game, as many people were quick to point out after England had failed to win, was only a friendly. This second meeting was a European Championship match. And England, now under Ron Greenwood, were enjoying a very impressive run of success at home and abroad.

In the end it was a game in which both teams definitely had, and missed, good chances. It was also a very fair result on the day and one which gave further proof that Ireland has a good and ever-improving international team. I was very proud of our display, as I am sure all Irishmen were.

For Arsenal, I was getting more and more involved in goal-scoring positions because I was pushing forward and had the confidence to shoot from distance. But our first ten games left us in ninth position in the table, out of the League Cup and looking towards Europe with increased excitement and hope.

Our opening game, and for most of us our first game, in Europe was against the highly rated East German side Loko-motive Leipzig who came to Highbury intent on making life difficult for us. This was something we were to experience time and again as our various European draws seemed to pair us with one Iron Curtain outfit after another.

One thing is for sure. My idea of this glorious and exciting European football was gradually dimmed. I imagined playing the Real Madrids and Barcelonas, Ajax and Hamburg. Instead we faced a succession of limb-chopping hard-men, past-masters at the one-attack, one-goal system. In short, about as colourful and exciting as a wet night.

Leipzig were well drilled, tough and determined. But grip-ping and entertaining they were not. No goals at half-time led to a little anxiety in the dressing-room. But, encouraged to carry on playing our own game no matter what, we finally nailed them. And they cracked.

Frank scored twice and Alan Sunderland's goal made it a pretty unassailable 3–0 first-leg lead. My European debut, even if I did have to hobble off to be replaced by Steve Gatting, ended in triumph. But not an awful lot of magic!

Ironically, out in East Germany we murdered them. Forced to attack in order to wipe out our impressive lead, Leipzig could not hold our attack and even their goal in our 4–1 win was an own-goal by Frank. Not that he worried – he scored two of our four to make it a rare type of 'hat-trick'.

So, safely through the first hurdle, we envisaged drawing one of the big and attractive European names in the second round. What did we get? An even harder bunch of East European storm-troopers called Hajduk Split from Yugoslavia. By the time we'd finished with them we learned a few lessons about the hardness of European competition . . . and I received my first 'continental' red card!

A partisan 30,000 crowd greeted us, if that is the right word, when we arrived for the first leg of that Hajduk tie. I was credited with my first goal in Europe in the first half, although David O'Leary touched in my shot. But goals by Cop and Djordjevic put them 2–1 up at the interval. And it was a hard old game by any standards.

It already worried them that we had scored an 'away' goal. So you can imagine how frustrated they became when they could not add to their lead throughout the second half. We had every reason to be happy on our flight home.

John Kosmina, who came over from Australia to try his fortunes in the League, learned more that night than at any other time of his career. In all that season, he only made one appearance in the First Division. That was as substitute for David Price in the opening game at home to Leeds.

It is some indication of how thin on the ground our squad was outside the recognized first team. When John's contract was eventually cancelled in March 1979, he left Arsenal with the unusual distinction of having played in more European games than League games. Because he came on as substitute when we met Hajduk for the second leg at Highbury, replacing the hacked and hobbling Mark Heeley, another lad possibly a bit raw for the roughness of our guests from Yugoslavia.

That was the night when I pushed aside my marker – he all but stepped inside my shorts – and received the red card from a referee who had clearly reached the end of his patience . . .

weary, no doubt of having to award me one free kick after another.

My marker went too, leaving ten-a-side to war it out in front of more than 40,000 bemused customers, people who suddenly discovered that, when compared with Hajduk, the League's most defensive teams appeared positively reckless.

I was sick about being sent off. The lads battled away, but I could not see them scoring the single goal that would put us into the third round. But I reckoned without big Willie Young.

When all seemed lost, the big Scot moved up to the edge of their area and cleverly lobbed in a loose ball. For such a big man, the chip-shot was a delicate and deliberate one because Willie saw that the goalkeeper was off his line. To our delight and relief, the ball dropped in under the bar with goalkeeper Budincevic wearing an expression of sheer horror.

At that stage, one of his team-mates completely lost his head. He knew that it was too late to save the game and that all their clattering and hanging on had been in vain. In the end the referee had no alternative but to send him off.

So we went through on the controversial 'away goals counting double' rule – or, to be more specific, by the skin of our teeth.

We were now enjoying what the press and punters describe as a 'cup run'. And with our cup record from the previous season, we began to believe that there was not a team left in the competition capable of attempting to frustrate us as much as Leipzig and Hajduk had.

How wrong can you be!

Back on the League front, we were moving up the table with increasing speed. From fifteenth on 26 August to fifth on 4 November . . . and there we stayed for five weeks before a David Price goal to beat Liverpool at Highbury followed by a 0–0 draw at Norwich broke the barrier. We were back in the top four.

Our form at this stage was superb. The atmosphere inside the club was such that everyone wanted to get in and get on with the job as early as possible. We felt united as a squad, confident in the ability of Don Howe and convinced that maybe, after all, our pre-season fears concerning the title were nothing more than pessimism, born of repeated disappointments.

The results, and the headlines, told their own story. But the day that stood out from the whole League programme was 23 December when we made the short trip to White Hart Lane for the eagerly awaited 'derby' match with Spurs. It turned out to be a very happy Christmas present for us and a nightmare for Keith Burkinshaw and his players. We won 5–0, a result that nobody in the world would have predicted, and I scored one of the best goals of my career, bending the ball with the outside of my left foot from the left-hand side of the area.

The only sour note of that period was the end of our European interest. As if to punish us for some unknown transgression, the draw paired us with Red Star Belgrade, another Yugoslavian collection of entertainers and wags. By this time I was sick to death of hearing about the great attraction of playing in Europe.

Belgrade was cold and unfriendly. We lost an unmemorable game 1–0 which I had to watch because of my ban from the sending off against Hajduk. But at Highbury we gave them a real hammering . . . yet went out of the UEFA Cup.

That was one of the most important lessons we learned. Nobody was in the least bit surprised when Red Star put up the shutters. Even the 41,000 crowd was resigned to a night on which Arsenal would set about breaking down a very tight defence and attempt to score two goals. But the way they caught us with a sucker-punch, and went on to do the same to WBA en route to the actual Final gave us all a new view of what European competition is all about.

How we failed to bury them is beyond me. But Red Star dug in and would not be pulled out. Once again I had to sit and shuffle my feet because of suspension. And once again Arsenal began with Mark Heeley and eventually replaced him with John Kosmina.

When Alan Sunderland finally broke the deadlock in the second half the whole ground sensed that total victory, and a place in the last eight, was only a matter of minutes away. But that was when Red Star struck out, with speed, skill and deadly accuracy. When they did attack they were very sharp and very dangerous.

153

Pat Jennings had no chance with the vicious drive belted past him by Savic just before the end – a shattering blow, especially after seeing Malcolm come on as a substitute for Graham Rix and promptly put the ball in the net only for it to be disallowed.

We got over the disappointment of Red Star's shock win and looked forward to the New Year with very real optimism. Sitting in the top four and ready and eager for another crack at the FA Cup, we were better off than most clubs when the weather turned truly Arctic.

Arsenal's excellent under-soil heating rescued a large percentage of our games while the rest of the country froze up. I became aware of repeated moans from a number of managers about how the weather, and the way it was interrupting the programme, was upsetting their players and destroying the rhythm of their teams.

I have never understood this. As I see it I train during the week in order to do my job. But I do not work in the dark. Usually I have a fairly good idea if our game has a chance of being played or if it is likely to be called off. Of course there are those games which are scrubbed at the last minute because of late pitch inspections. But even so, all this does to me is make me all the keener to get ready for the next week.

The more games I miss the more restless I become to play. And I imagine the majority of footballers are the same. After a two-week lay-off I am itching to get involved in a five-a-side training match, let alone a First Division fixture.

Maybe a team's momentum can be partly interrupted by bad weather and postponements. But it still comes down to whether or not a team is good enough. If you have the players you will come through in the end no matter how long the season takes to complete.

Anyone who blames the elements for his shortcomings is unlikely to be that much better even if the sun is splitting the trees.

At the half-way stage the season had already been a successful and eventful one. Our young team was moulding well and growing up together. If anything, I believe Rotherham did us a favour. After that defeat we came to our senses with a jolt and knew that a team of our standing should never go down the way we did that August night. That defeat provided us with a platform, a basement from which to climb.

Considering the lack of strength-in-depth in the club I am convinced that we did well in Europe. But I must add that I never enjoyed playing in Europe. It was much better imagining how it would be because when I came in contact with the kickers and cynics from behind the Iron Curtain, they knocked a lot of the magic, and dreams, out of my head.

Nevertheless, I was never more happy and never more convinced that, with one or two more class players, we could really win something big.

As we entered the New Year we were destined to go all the way back to Wembley and figure in one of the most talked about Cup Finals in football history. But our initial FA Cup ties indicated anything but a finale that was to prove the highlight of my professional life.

15

The Press Problem

The voice on the other end of my telephone was that of Kevin Moseley of the *Daily Mirror*. He explained to me that Arsenal chairman Denis Hill-Wood, had said that the club was prepared to do everything possible to keep me at Highbury and that before the paper could carry the story it was necessary for me to comment.

I accepted Kevin's point and told him that the chairman had not spoken to me about the matter, but that in any case it had always been my intention to play abroad.

He thanked me for helping him out and I was more than happy to oblige . . . until I read the paper the next day.

The headline read to the effect 'Liam Brady says no to Arsenal' an exclusive by Kevin Moseley. Now I had said 'No' to nobody, I only gave the reporter an answer to his question, a specific request on his part for me to make a comment.

Yet by the time my two sentences were converted into a story it had become an 'exclusive' – some exclusive! I always believed that such a claim could only be made if someone specifically singled out a paper and gave his 'story' to that paper and no other.

I was angry and I was disappointed. The story did nothing to enhance my popularity at Highbury. And all I got in return for trying to help a guy do his job was trouble.

These are words that I hope every youngster who hopes to make it in the game reads and reads carefully. It is vital that you find out the men you can trust, and those you cannot trust, in the media.

There is no hard and fast rule about what to do when confronted by a pack of journalists. Nor can I provide you with a list of things to say and not to say. But I do stress this – think about the whole business of press relations and make some important decisions. Choose your contacts, if indeed you want any, and choose your words very carefully.

I am not the first footballer to write about the press. And I am sure that I shall not be the last. So I want to make it clear that I do not have any great fear of the media, nor do I entertain any grudges or bitterness.

But I do believe that it is very important for a young player to understand the importance of the media, the influence newspapers have within the game and the good, and bad, they can do.

That example concerning Kevin Moseley is just one I selected to illustrate how the conversation which appears the most harmless can be turned into something entirely different and more sinister by the time it goes through the national newspaper 'machine'.

Having said that, I also believe that clubs are just as much to blame for the lousy relationship that exists between press and players in Britain.

There is no doubt that the press and the clubs need each other. Both are in business, both need to sell something to keep going, and their inter-dependence makes the secrecy and whispered stories all the more absurd.

The sad truth is that there is a lack of trust on the part of the players and, I am sure, on the part of many reporters.

I, for one, would never dream of going out among the reporters after an Arsenal match to discuss the pros and cons of the ninety minutes. Why? Because I could never be certain how my words would be interpreted, where they would be used and how they would be twisted to suit the purposes of some faceless 'sub' on a desk, anxious to find a story to suit his pet headline of the evening.

In short, I don't trust them! And that is a bloody tragedy because I need the press as much as the press needs people like me.

So where do we all go wrong? Why does this trust gap exist?

One reason, as I see it, is that newspapers do not actually

157

report matches as they happen. To be fair, the likes of the *Times* and the *Telegraph* certainly do. And the *Guardian* enjoys selecting some weird theme all of its own and pursuing that, but it usually gets across the guts of the match all the same. No, it's the so-called populars that annoy me.

You can pick up a copy of the *Sun* and read 'match report by so-and-so'. But when you read the damn thing it is nothing more than a whole screed on the antics of an individual or an incident in the game.

As far as I am concerned, all these boring, meaningless quotes that they seem to believe are so important are the root cause of the problem. It seems that papers do not trust their reporters to give an accurate report of a game any more. The man with the job of sitting in the press box and watching the game has also got to find out what everyone else 'thought' about what he has seen before he is allowed to write his report!

To me this is an insult to the reporter and to the fans. The people at the game know what happened, and those who were not there want to know what happened. People giving opinions of what happened in a particular incident are not as important.

I must stress that this is only my opinion. I know many players who enjoy regular communications with the press. They love going straight out after a game and answering questions. I do not.

If I believe that, for example, the supporters should know how I feel about a certain situation then I will relate my feelings, accurately and truthfully, through the medium of the newspapers or radio or television, depending on who is interested. But as for the banalities of after-match quotes, I have no time for this side of reporting.

My first experiences with the national press happened after I made my debut for Arsenal, as a substitute, against Birmingham City. Things were pretty grey at Highbury around that time, and the reporters latched on to me because I played well and obviously provided them with something to write about that was new and fresh.

But after the initial excitement of being the centre of attention I began to notice how the whole business worked. I saw what was written about other players and wondered why it was that so few of the papers actually carried the reports of matches I expected them to carry.

Then the common sense aspect of it struck me. Newspapers are competitive. They must attract readers. And clearly they do not believe they can do so without glossing up the simple facts to suit their own ends. They need sensations all the time – even when there are no sensations.

And if a reporter wrote something nice about me, it seemed as if he believed I should be eternally grateful, that I should agree every time he wanted to write some garbage to fill an expanse of white space on the back page of his paper.

Reporting is not my job. I do not have to work and live under the pressures reporters exist under. If I did I might well write the very same type of waffle. But it seems to me that the papers ought to give the players more credit for their intelligence than they do.

We know all about the average impression of the soccer pro – but just as we have idiots in our profession, so the media have their share of idiots also.

As I have already said, I do believe that papers maintain the level of magic and excitement that exists in the game. The game needs the publicity. The fans demand the communication and the information. They want, and need, an everlasting link with their club and their players.

All the more reason, therefore, why papers – and clubs – should give more thought to these people. To clubs they are fans and represent revenue. To the papers they are readers. But they still represent revenue.

If you took the newspaper element out of the game, everybody would notice the terrible void. And I am happy in the knowledge that the vast majority of writers are, in this country certainly, the very top of their tree.

But it seems that the handful of reporters who feel quite at home being ruthless and basically unfair to the men they interview are the ones who stick in your mind . . . and make you suspicious of everyone.

This is the area where I stress that young up and coming players must make up their own minds. If you are prepared to talk to people who repeatedly misuse your quotes then you deserve all the problems you get. Be selective and think before you speak.

Never underestimate the power of the written word.

Newspapers have tremendous power and influence within the game. I believe that, if papers decide to attack a certain subject, their campaign carries great weight at FA and Football League levels.

And it is this power and influence that worries me. The day Sammy Nelson dropped his shorts after scoring an equalizing, and point-winning, goal against Coventry City at Highbury, he sparked off a vicious and totally unfair campaign aimed at doing great damage to his professional career.

Certain papers claimed that he did what he did as an insult to a section of the fans who barracked him earlier for deflecting in City's goal. This was completely untrue and terribly unfair.

I played in the same team as Sammy. I know the man. And I know the Arsenal fans. They did not have a go at him and Sammy, a natural prankster, dropped his shorts as nothing more than a fun gesture. I am not saying he was clever, nor that he did not deserve some type of disciplinary action. But, for God's sake, it hardly merited the sort of nasty stories which claimed that he should never be allowed to play for Arsenal again.

What gives these people the right to guess at a man's reasons for doing something and then verbally maul him on the basis of that assumption? I cannot see any justification for what the papers did to Sammy during that incident. They screamed for his head at a time when we were trying to prepare for an FA Cup Final.

Were they really so concerned with the good image of the game? Were they so outraged that they believed the player should have been thrown out of his job? Or were they, as I suspect, more concerned with filling more white space? And would the whole nonsense have been blown up as big as it was if we had not been on our way to face Manchester United at Wembley?

The FA and the League appear to fear certain newspaper campaigns. In some ways this is a good thing. The democratic right of the media to attack what is bad is healthy and a great help to society as a whole. But when such power is abused, great harm can be done.

By the time Sammy Nelson had paid his fines and served his suspensions – and both were in the plural – his flash of backside had cost him more than the average offender is fined for indecent exposure in a public place. But would the situation have reached such dramatic proportions without the insistent newspaper articles which refused to let the business die?

All of which makes me wonder what the papers want from the game, and from the people who play it. Do they really want to report football and footballers, or do they want to dig the dirt whenever possible, in an attempt to tempt you and me to buy their paper as we dash for the commuter train instead of the paper we usually buy?

Beware, also, of the Fleet Street 'jungle drum'.

I remember talking to Steve Curry of the *Daily Express* one afternoon and discussing Alan Ball. Curry wanted to write an article as a preview to our game against Southampton. It was to be the first time I would play against Bally since his transfer from Arsenal to The Dell.

I told him how much I looked forward to the game and added how helpful Alan had been to me during the early part of my career. It all seemed simple enough. A direct conversation between Liam Brady of Arsenal and Mr Curry of the *Express*.

But the next day I read the story – with my quotes, word for word, in Kevin Moseley's article in the *Mirror*. He did nothing wrong in terms of representation. But I was disappointed in Curry. I trusted him and gave him his interview. I can only assume that he then gave it to Moseley and whoever else got in touch to swop daily snippets. If this is competitive journalism then I'll eat my shin pads.

Of course you also get the extremely funny side of the game through the papers. When we played England in the European Championship tie in Dublin, David Miller of the *Express* wrote an appalling article which said that England should win by at least 4–0!

Now I don't know what Miller thought Ron Greenwood had in terms of a team but I do know that he put those England lads under terrible and unfair pressure. Saying, in effect, that they would be failures if they did not hammer us out of sight on our own ground.

The fact that they were damn lucky to draw with us at Wembley not so long before appeared to have escaped Miller's expert attention.

But what really angered all of the Irish lads was the way this arrogant man wrote about us as if we were donkeys and mugs, a team containing a vast majority of First Division footballers.

The game, a close-fought affair, ended 1–1, and this was a good result for England, all things considered. So when I emerged from the dressing-room afterwards I saw all the press lads waiting and I shouted out: 'Where is that ******* Harry Miller?'

Poor Harry, one of the most respected reporters in the business, looked at me as if I had shot him and spluttered in shock, asking what he was supposed to have done.

In my anger, I had yelled out for the wrong Miller and had to make a loud and immediate apology to Harry. David Miller, however, was nowhere to be seen. And this, also, angered me.

He had written his clever article, insulting one team and embarrassing the other. Now he did not have to account for his totally incorrect 'expert' opinion. No, that was left to the players on the England side who, in the eyes of many fans who take the *Daily Express*, had failed to meet Miller's 4–0 minimum triumph.

There are hundreds of tales worth recounting where players have been sold down the river by reporters and where reporters have been given duff information by players. And it is a sad state of affairs.

It definitely is a matter of trust, or the lack of it.

But then you see stories about Stanley Bowles, George Best, Malcolm Macdonald . . . lots of star players, who seem unable to keep out of the headlines. It seems to me that they get what they deserve. If they are so unhappy about what is written about them, why do they complain after they have willingly spoken with reporters? Such moans usually fall on deaf ears within the game.

But every now and again you come across the sort of incident that not only sours you but makes you all the more determined to keep your mouth shut and your opinions firmly out of the press.

I remember being in the middle of conversation one afternoon when somebody lurched towards me and announced: 'God, Liam, have you heard . . . Malcolm Macdonald has been killed in a car crash.'

The news hit me like a boxer's punch. I was numb, speechless and sick to my stomach. What made it worse was the fact that it was a day off for the players and I had not seen Malcolm since the day before, so it was all entirely possible.

Then I remembered the fact that Malcolm had that long drive from North London to Bedfordshire to his home – a ninety-minute drive up the M1 twice a day. More ammunition to make credible this awful news.

As it turned out, a crank had phoned the newspapers and told them that Malcolm had been involved in a fatal accident. As it happened, there was a Mr Macdonald killed somewhere in the south of England in a car crash that same day, and thus arose the confusion. By the end of the day it almost had disastrous consequences . . . all because of a reporter's thoughtlessness.

Unknown to any of us, a certain reporter, who for the sake of his professional credibility shall remain nameless, had the heartless unprofessionalism to phone Malcolm's home and ask his pregnant wife if the reports concerning the accident and death were true!

Needless to say Julie Macdonald was terribly shocked and upset. All the more so because it just so happened that Malcolm had driven to Bucks on business that very day.

Our jokes to Malcolm about him looking remarkably good for a ghost when he arrived for training the next day went very flat when he told us exactly why he was wearing a black look and why he was gunning for a certain Fleet Street reporter.

He did not, as we feared, wring this individual's neck. But nor did he ever speak to him again, nor his paper for a very long time.

This is where the need to get the story first gets out of hand. The whole situation was unnecessary and could have had terrible consequences. Luckily it came to nothing, but for the lads at Highbury, the whole newspaper industry suffered a few days of shabby reputation until match day took over our thoughts.

But then I must ask why clubs seem so reluctant to answer simple, straight questions and why they seem obsessed with this 'no comment' nonsense. Nothing is more certain to fire a reporter's curiosity than the 'no comment' get-out.

The daft thing is that there is usually nothing worth commenting about in the first place and days of speculation and dubious headlines can be avoided by telling the truth.

In this respect I blame the clubs, not the press.

This is a frustrating country for ducking and dodging and giving stupid answers to important questions. The fans pay for football's existence. They have a right to know what is going on in the club they do so much to support.

But up to the recent change in the situation, players found a clause in their contracts banning them from speaking with the press without prior permission. This was, of course, farcical, especially in a democracy. Yet managers were allowed to stand in front of television cameras and criticize.

The answer is simple, and it is being proved to be as such every week in Europe and the United States. If manager and players attended an after-match press conference for five or ten minutes then most of the speculation and rubbish would disappear.

The essential thing would be to ensure that this conference was the only one, and that it was available for all the press at the same time. This would make the reporters' lives much easier and clear up many misunderstandings . . . and the awful lack of trust we seem to feel towards each other at the moment.

16

The Joy of Making
Amends

When people talk about the 1979 FA Cup Final in terms of those dramatic closing minutes, my memories usually go further back, back to Sheffield and an ice-rink of a pitch and a game which took 570 minutes and sixteen goals to resolve.

There is no doubt that the Final itself was a thrilling affair, without ever achieving the level of a classic match. But to win the Cup a team must win a minimum of six games. Arsenal had to play – and come through – no less than eleven ties before capturing the trophy which had eluded us the year before.

Any way you look at it, this was a marvellous achievement and one in which I am very proud to have been involved.

Even now, whenever anybody mentions the expression 'cup tie', I don't think of Manchester United, nor of Wolves, whom we beat in the semi-final. No, I think of Sheffield Wednesday, a once mighty First Division club reduced to associate League membership and the Third Division, who rose to heights that even their manager, the vastly experienced Jack Charlton, could not have expected.

Wednesday always matched us for effort, nearly always for skill and kept us on the ropes for five unforgettable matches which finished with both sets of players on first-name terms and an aggregate score of 9–7!

Personally I shall never forget those games. Because during them I learned to recognize just about every aspect of a cup tie – the mental pendulum which swings initially towards the under-dog, then across to the favourite, then back sharply to the under-dog before moving steadily towards the favourite with each successive match.

That is how it was against Wednesday. Our satisfaction at gaining a replay from the first tie at Hillsborough, their delight and our relief after the replay, their fire and our determination not to look mugs in the third game, and finally their realization that their chance had gone. That with every extra match we were able to put our superior skills and know-how into operation. And they were running out of surprises to throw us.

I have no doubt that the dreadful weather of that winter played a major part in making the Cup programme a weird and disjointed affair, with teams over-lapping their ties, playing fourth-round replays while others were facing sixth-round replays.

It is astonishing that players are asked to perform in conditions such as those we experienced before and after that Christmas.

Rugby players, golfers, tennis players, cricketers . . . even racehorses are allowed to postpone activity during the type of frozen, Arctic winter of 1978–79. But footballers? We come under a different heading. And it is wrong.

People pay hard-earned money to see good football, not grown men skidding and sliding around a dangerous rink of ruts, ice and snow while factors such as skill and ability are reduced to levels of pure farce.

Aside from the fact that such conditions are physically dangerous to people whose profession carries a strong risk of injury anyway, playing on 'impossible' pitches brings down the standards all round and leads to false results in certain games.

The League programme was also badly hit. In some parts of the country the game ground to a total halt, doubtless costing the clubs involved a lot of money. But in these cases it was absolutely impossible to play because of snow, in some cases knee high.

We ended 1978 with a 3–1 home win over Birmingham City, a result which held us in fourth place and set up everyone for the beginning of the Cup programme.

The third round 'opener' against Wednesday took place on 6 January. It seemed strange for a Third Division club to have such a beautiful stadium as Hillsborough. But then Wednes-

166

day were still trying to get used to their fall from the dizzy heights of the 1960s when they were First Division runners-up, playing in Europe and beaten FA Cup Finalists in 1966.

Tradition and history are all very interesting. But the reality from our point of view was a difficult Cup tie away from home, played on an ice-rink in front of more than 33,000 people, the vast majority of whom wanted to see us beaten. And, whatever their background, the Sheffield Wednesday we faced that day were an outfit lying sixteenth in the Third Division while we were fourth in the First.

So when Alan Sunderland gave us a first-half lead, things were going according to expectations. We anticipated a tough task and Wednesday gave us one. They chased everything, hustled us into errors and gave their success-starved fans a reminder of bygone days.

The equalizer, which sparked off what will surely go down in history as one of the great FA Cup battles, was scored by Jeff Johnson. And, to be honest, we were perfectly happy with a Highbury replay. Maybe that very attitude was our first mistake.

They came to London on 9 January . . . and gave us the fright of our lives.

Roger Wylde put them ahead in the first half, and as the game progressed we became more and more anxious. Wednesday, far from accepting their draw at home and a healthy share of the Highbury gate receipts as their Cup 'lot', were confident they could beat us.

Now, of course, we were under pressure. Because as the home side we were expected to win. An away draw was a form of success. Anything short of a home win would bring scorn on our heads. And we knew it.

Not even the backing we received from a near 38,000 crowd appeared to throw Wednesday out of their stride. They were composed, strong and determined. And we were only a matter of seconds away from being dumped out of a competition we eventually went on to win.

When it seemed that nothing would penetrate their defence, Frank Stapleton got up brilliantly at the far post, knocked the ball down and I stuck it past the defiant Chris Turner.

The crowd went wild. Not with joy but, like the Arsenal players, with sheer relief. But even then, Wednesday maintained their composure and survived extra-time, giving Pat Jennings a few things to do in the process.

It was two days later when weeks of negotiations were completed and Brian Talbot, one of the men instrumental in our Wembley defeat in May 1978, signed for Arsenal for £450,000.

We all welcomed Brian's arrival because he added strength to our midfield and gave us a better midfield balance by operating on the right. David Price did well for us there, but Brian was the stronger of the two and David moved position to accommodate the new arrival.

Talbot was quickly swept up in all the excitement of our Wednesday saga. But he did not actually play in any of the ties.

He made his Arsenal debut that Saturday in a 2–1 win over Champions Forest, a game which attracted more than 52,000 fans. We were really going some at this stage and people actually began talking in terms of a League and Cup 'double'. To the older hands at Highbury it must have seemed like turning back the clock to 1970 and 1971.

Filbert Street, Leicester, was selected as the neutral venue of our second replay with Wednesday, and a thrilling, open game ended 2–2 after extra time. Once again I got on the score-sheet, along with Alan Sunderland. But it was a little ironic that Brian Hornsby, an ex-Arsenal player, should score both of their goals.

With the weather so bad, League football was almost at a standstill. But with their famous hot-air balloon, Leicester continued to play hosts as we shaped up for the fourth meeting on 17 January. By now the game was truly national news. It gave the press a field-day with both camps being quoted, injury stories by the dozen and the usual pre-match build-up material.

But we began to sense that Wednesday were running out of steam. And having got so far, we had no intention of being made to look fools. Bad enough to face a replay. But the prospect of going out after failing to beat a Third Division team at four attempts was something none of us could stomach.

The fourth game was a six-goal heart-stopper which kept the

168

frozen fans on their toes for another 120 minutes. Frank Stapleton struck two good goals and big Willie Young was also on target. But that man Hornsby continued to haunt us, scoring their third goal from the penalty spot. I felt all the worse as he tucked it away, because I missed a penalty at the stage when they led 1–0.

Although we could hardly believe it, we had to meet for a fifth time. And by now, after this many Cup ties, we felt as if we ought to be facing the semi-final. Yet neither side was any nearer to the fourth round!

This time we made no mistake. Steve Gatting and Frank Stapleton gave us a two-goal advantage before the interval, and Wednesday, who had matched us blow for blow, were unable to muster another counter-punch.

They deserved the standing ovation of the 30,000 crowd that night. But if their Cup season was over, ours was just beginning. Now I felt a sense of the inevitable. Surely no team would go through all of what we had overcome and at the end of it fail to win the Cup?

Brian Talbot replaced Gatting for the fourth-round tie, at home to Notts County on 27 January. And in complete contrast, this game was something of an anti-climax. We won easily, more easily than the 2–0 scoreline indicates. What did add to the day was Talbot scoring our second goal, immediately giving those sharp lads in Fleet Street an angle they could play with as long as we stayed in the Cup.

Was Brian Talbot going to become the first man to win a Cup winners' medal with the team he had helped to beat in the previous Final? Looked at in the light of probability, most people would have said: 'No chance, the odds are against it.' But football is not about theory and odds. It is about people and their ambitions and their determination to achieve those ambitions.

We all wanted to make up for the bitter disappointment of losing to Ipswich. Brian wanted to go back to Wembley and win another medal because he is a professional, not because it happened to fit into some nice pattern of events likely to go down in a future book of 'Football Feats'.

On the League scene we continued to press towards the top.

Two Alan Sunderland goals beat Manchester United at Old Trafford, and it was just as well. Because local rivalry must never be underestimated. And our 1978 Cup disappointments coupled with Tottenham regaining their First Division status shifted the initial spotlight across North London, to White Hart Lane.

Keith Burkinshaw's courage in signing the World Cup Argentinians Osvaldo Ardiles and Ricardo Villa for a reported £750,000 created such excitement and such a stir in our game that all eyes seemed to be focused on Spurs at the start of the season.

I have heard two sides of the argument – the one that says importing foreign players limits the chances of young players born and bred in England, and the one that welcomes new faces and new blood on the basis that interest is stimulated and people come to matches.

Me? I believe that if British players want to, and can, go and play their football abroad, it would be the height of hypocrisy for us to attempt to ban foreign players from coming over to Britain.

In any case, the Treaty of Rome stipulates that there must be freedom of movement between Common Market nations, so that opens the doors to and from most of Europe's top football countries.

The fact that Spurs grabbed the headlines at the beginning of season 1978–79 by signing those two lads must have been good for the club, the fans and whole team. People who might not have gone otherwise made a point of going just to see the two South Americans in action. That cannot possibly be bad for the game.

Arsenal were linked with two foreign players – the gifted Dutch internationals Johan Neeskens and Ruud Krol – but nothing came of it. Some people claimed that we, as a club, would not entertain foreign players. But this was rubbish. I believe that Arsenal would have had no hesitation about a foreign player if they had really wanted him. But, frankly, it was decided that the squad would not benefit simply through the introduction of a 'foreigner' to keep the fans happy. Arsenal is too big a club to go in for trend-following of this nature.

170

What was happening, of course, was that top clubs discovered it was possible to sign an international player of, say,
Arnold Muhren's calibre for a lot less than it would cost to buy
a player of a lot less ability from a Second Division club.

League clubs seemed hell-bent on self-destruction, lifting
transfer prices to farcical heights. All that happened was that
players, held at unreasonable prices by their clubs, were
helped considerably by independent tribunals, and an influx of
Poles and Yugoslavians added some new colour to the League
scene, usually for comparative bargain-basement prices.

All of which added to the validity of our claim to be one of the
best teams in the land. We required no gimmicks to recapture
the spotlight. Results and growing consistency, plus the very
sound signing of Brian Talbot, gave Arsenal credibility as con-
tenders for the 'double'. At least the fans thought so and they
turned up to support this cause.

But still there was the woeful weather to contend with. And
this brought into action that extraordinary soccer organ – the
Pools Panel.

I will never understand the need for so comical a body, even
accepting the big money wrapped up in football pools. One
glance at their blunders is enough to make everyone roll up
with laughter – predictions that sometimes made nonsense of
the whole season.

The whole daft business was summed up for me in a cartoon
I saw which portrayed a manager standing over a player who
was laying back on a treatment couch, staring anxiously at the
large hammer in his manager's hand.

Manager: 'I'm sorry about this Fred, but according to the
Pools Panel we lost 1–0 and you broke a leg.'

Idiotic it may have been, but that cartoon represented
everything about the Panel which I see as farcical. And
although the press often like to make out that players become
either upset or elated after reading the Panel's verdicts for a
football-free Saturday, the truth is that the vast majority of us
either ignore the whole stupid affair or view it as a source of
light amusement.

It was to this background of weather-induced chaos that we
approached what was undoubtedly our toughest tie of the

whole Cup run – and in that I include the Final. We were drawn away to Nottingham Forest, a game which, at best, would leave us with a second crack at them in a replay.

And, although we were by now lying second in the League, teams behind us had games in hand and we knew our true standing in a highly competitive League. This means that we expected one hell of a hard ninety minutes at The City Ground, and that is precisely what Brian Clough's excellent team gave us.

But, against all predictions by the so-called experts, we beat Forest on their own pitch, a tremendous result achieved in the face of tremendous pressure. That we were lucky goes without saying. Pat Jennings was inspired, the defence rode its good fortune as Forest launched concentrated assaults. But we held firm, shut them down, kept a close eye on the dangerous John Robertson . . . then knocked the wind out of their stomachs with a goal from Frank Stapleton.

If there was one moment when I went against my previous beliefs, and accepted that Cup winners' names are written on the Cup from the start of the season, it was after we had beaten Forest.

I cannot imagine a tougher draw than that one at that time. The fact that we got the breaks when we needed them most, then possessed the guts to go back at them and snatch total victory, only served to convince us that nobody left in the competition was good enough to prevent us from winning it. We had faced the best and knocked them out.

As so often happens in football, the Cup draw paired us with a team we were due to play around the same time in a League game. We went down to Southampton on 3 March and lost 2–0, knowing that we had to return to The Dell on 19 March for an FA Cup quarter-final. Forest were out, but it seemed there were still tough ties left in the hat.

By this stage in my career I believed that I had encountered just about every nerve-racking, frightening occasion that a player can face – League debut, first international match, England *v.* Ireland, Cup semi-finals and finals – all the traditional gut-tighteners.

But nothing can compare with the butterflies I suffered on 18

Exchanging 'words' with my marker from Hajduk Split in the return UEFA
Cup match at Highbury. We were both sent off and I was annoyed with
myself for losing my patience

The opening match of the 1978/79 season. A great start for me against
Leeds United (*here with Brian Flynn in opposition*) – I scored both goals in the
2–2 home draw

(*Above*) twisting my way through the French defence and (*below*) scoring the goal which beat France 1–0 in Dublin

Letting fly against England in our 1–1 draw at Wembley in 1976 – an unforgettable night

We drew against England again in Dublin, but this time the stakes were the European Championship

The historic first meeting between Ireland and Northern Ireland in Dublin ended 0–0

Back to Wembley again soon after winning the 1979 FA Cup but this time we lost 3–1 to Liverpool in the Charity Shield

March when I stepped up to receive the 'Player of the Year' award at the London Hilton Hotel.

To be absolutely honest, a lot of that evening is lost in a fog of congratulations and handshakes and excitement. Because no matter what award you receive as a player, when your fellow pros select you as their choice, then there is no higher award.

Who better to judge the true merits of a barrister or doctor than members of their own professions? The same applies in all professions. And football is certainly no exception.

When the Football Writers name you as their Footballer of the Year, it is a great honour because every member of this long-established body casts a vote and the whole process is entirely democratic. You know that the majority of writers have selected you, a selection based on how you performed when they saw you in action.

But they are writers and you are a player. Their selection is made on the basis of how they judge the game, and the men who play it, from a press-box point of view. With all due respect, the writers are up there, not down on the pitch, knowing every side of a man's performance, when he is hiding yet appearing to be in the thick of things, when he is really hurt and when he is shamming and so on.

No misunderstandings, please! I am not for one moment trying to take anything away from the Footballer of the Year award. It is a marvellous award to win. But ask any player and I'll bet that he will choose the PFA award – the pro selected by the pros.

People had suggested that I was among the hopefuls before I went along to the Hilton. But when I realized I had won, I was very moved by the reactions of the other Arsenal players. I wanted to find another way of saying what every player seems to say on such occasions – that the award was won by his team-mates as much as it was won by him. But I couldn't find the words so in the end I just made a short, straightforward acceptance speech.

When a player wins this award, his team-mates are genuinely chuffed because they know that without them he would not have won it, and therefore they consider the award reflects well upon the whole team. And so it does.

173

I did have a good season. I was scoring goals, keeping my head up all the time looking for options and could feel the confidence running through me – a far cry from those previous seasons which, when I thought about it, were only a matter of moments past.

Winning that award added to my confidence and made me aware of just what my standing was in the professional game. I am not a fool. I knew that my ability was rated, both by fellow pros and by the fans and media. But the award capped it all – answered every question I wanted to ask but usually felt too shy to ask.

How far had I really come since leaving Dublin? According to professional footballers, I had come one hell of a way. But Irish caps apart, I had nothing to show for it, no winners' medals.

Which led me nicely into our quarter-final tie against Southampton. The whole season would be complete if we could only wipe away the memory of Ipswich and 1978. Yes, it is damn hard to reach Wembley in successive seasons, but something kept telling me that we were up to it, that we were a better side and just destined to get there.

All the time Don Howe kept the magic in the air by varying training, working with us on every tiny problem that either he saw or we brought up. He never allowed the threat of boredom, monotony or anxiety to creep into the squad. We were swept along through a terrible winter by our own ambitions and convictions, and the coaching of one man.

Southampton played well and deserved the lead Austin Hayes gave them after the break. But their goalkeeper, Tony Gennoe, made one mistake and David Price pounced to equalize, earning us a Highbury replay that once again had seemed a lost hope.

It was amazing how often during that run that we came from having our backs against the wall to triumph, or earned one reprieve after another by sheer willpower, discipline and by following Howe's directive that you never give up until you are in the bath.

Two days later, on 21 March, we beat Southampton 2–0 at Highbury thanks to a couple of Alan Sunderland goals. But for

me it was something of a repeat nightmare as I suffered a liga-
ment injury and limped off to be replaced by Steve Walford.

For me, the after-match celebrations at reaching the semi-
final were tempered by the memory of my blunder before that
1978 final, how I played when I should have declared myself
unfit. I was hurt again, and the semi-final was coming up. I
had ten days.

I knew I would not be fit for the semi-final and when Terry
Neill asked me I said: 'No, I am definitely not available. I am
injured.' That was all he wanted to hear. And I believe that
this is all any manager wants to hear – a positive yes or no. It is
only when a player starts mumbling about 'maybes' and 'perhaps' that he encourages his employers, who undoubtedly
want him out there on the big day, to push and nudge him into
a position where he lets down everyone else in the side.

Once Terry Neill knew my decision, he selected his team,
with Steve Gatting in my place – and as it turned out, Steve
played a blinder.

The build-up to the semi-final was misleading. We took only
one point from three games while our opponents, Wolves,
while hardly on the crest of a wave, were certainly in a positive
frame of mind. The arrival of manager John Barnwell and his
assistant, Ritchie Barker, signalled the beginning of a remarkable fight-back at Molineux.

Wolves were, without doubt, one of the poorest sides in
Division One that season. Their confidence had gone and they
looked safe bets for the drop.

But Barnwell's enthusiasm lifted the players and put fire
back in their bellies. And as they climbed away from the relegation zone, they looked upon their Cup run almost as a bonus,
something extra to look forward to.

I kept reading bits and pieces which forecast an upset at
Villa Park, a Wolves victory to complete their fairy-tale reco-
very. But once again Howe, a Wolverhampton man by birth,
who still lives in that area, analysed their game and left the side
in no doubts as to what needed to be done.

With all due respect to the Arsenal fans, Villa Park seemed
two-thirds jammed with Midlanders – hardly surprising under
the circumstances – and it must have been as close to a home

game for Wolves as Stamford Bridge had been for Orient and Arsenal in 1978.

Semi-finals are rarely classic games. There is too much tension, too much at stake. It is worse, I imagine, to lose an FA Cup semi-final than it is to actually lose at Wembley. To get so near and fail must be agony.

So as I took my place on the sideline I felt nervous, more so than if I had been out there with the lads, keyed up and waiting to get on with the job. I do not enjoy being a spectator. There is always a feeling of frustration because you cannot contribute anything more than vocal encouragement in between rubbing your hands together, trying not to chew your nails and shuffling your feet under the bench.

That Saturday, 31 March, was an ideal football day. Unfortunately we did not see that much good football.

I watched Steve Gatting closely, hoping nerves would not ruin his game. He played a very good game in midfield. And any thoughts Wolves may have had about the side missing me in any way were quickly crushed.

In between the offsides, lofted clearances and hopeful punts from end to end in the wind, it was evident that Arsenal looked the more relaxed and more organized side. Really, Wolves had achieved so much in such a short space of time that they were unable to pace themselves mentally. It was as if they wanted it all to happen right away. And the longer the half went on, the more Arsenal took a grip in midfield.

Dave O'Leary and Willie Young snuffed out John Richards and Billy Rafferty who, in turn, did not receive the service from midfield to put their strengths to the best use. On the other hand, Alan Sunderland and Frank Stapleton kept the Wolves defence stretched.

Strange things happen in semi-finals. And I was worried that Wolves might snatch one goal. Why? Because it was the type of game which one goal could have settled.

Wolves were not playing well. But I wanted to see our first goal go in before feeling safe. After a score-less first half, Frank powered away from two challenges and fired past Paul Bradshaw to open the score. At that moment I knew we had done the impossible. We had returned to Wembley.

Alan Sunderland's second goal – a cheeky shot through the unfortunate Bradshaw's legs – gave the score-line a realistic look. Yet it was probably the most important goal Alan had scored in his career . . . and the one which gave him least pleasure.

Wolves was Alan's first club. He grew up with a large percentage of the lads whom he helped beat at Villa Park. And their disappointment and anger at their own poor performance hit him hard. He told me how much it upset him to see his former mates so dejected. And he was even in two minds about going across and commiserating with one or two of the players after the final whistle. It was Wolves's second losing FA Cup semi-final in six years and some of the older players were certainly feeling it.

That is the absolute measure of this competition. When compared with the League Cup it leaves the League's tournament miles behind in terms of prestige, tradition, excitement and world-wide reputation. I had suffered the empty feeling of coming away from Wembley a loser. But I believe that Hibbitt and his colleagues felt a damn sight worse for missing the opportunity of going to Wembley.

I felt strange, wandering among the lads afterwards. I did not have to get changed and did not need a bath. But I certainly helped myself to a swig or two of champagne!

I don't know what it is about reaching the Cup Final, but the moment you do so, you become the immediate target of everybody – well-wishers, threatening cranks, the media put you under a microscope, injuries normally treated as part and parcel of the daily routine are suddenly being described as 'crippling threat to Wembley hopes', and 'countdown agony for so-and-so'.

Even worse is the way referees seem to become more aware of your every word and gesture in games leading up to the big day.

On 3 April we played Coventry City at Highbury – hardly a game likely to lead to any great controversial incidents. But that is just what happened.

We were trailing at half-time to a goal that was supposed to have been deflected in off Sammy Nelson. So when Sammy

177

stormed up and equalized in the second half, he was so excited that he got carried away . . . and dropped his shorts to the crowd.

As I said earlier, I know that Sammy did that on impulse and because he was so pleased to have wiped out his first-half deflection. But the press went to town and one story actually tried to make out that the fans had been giving him a hard time after City had gone ahead, and that that he had deliberately shown them his backside in reply when he scored.

This was absolute rubbish and a disgraceful thing to write. But not only was Sammy fined and suspended by Arsenal, he received an even heavier dose of punishment from the authorities. Which just about sums them up. These people come down hard on silly, stupid and trivial matters yet rarely appear to be so sharp when it comes to players on the field who kick their way through one game after another.

Yet Sammy was hammered – twice – for something which I believe should have been wrapped up with a small fine and a rap on the knuckles.

As if that were not enough, Willie Young was then sent off in our match up at The Baseball Ground, Derby on 21 April. Understandably he was initially worried about missing the Final, but to this day we are all convinced that he was the victim of a mistake by the referee. Significantly, Willie did not miss Wembley!

I had returned to the side shortly after the semi-final, feeling tremendous after making the correct decision and even more tremendous at the prospect of going back and getting the chance to make up to everyone for the disaster of 1978.

I returned to the team for the 'derby' match against Spurs on 10 April when a Frank Stapleton goal was enough to give us a North London 'double'. Then we hammered poor Chelsea 5–2 after drawing up at West Brom. But uppermost in our minds – and I defy any player or manager to tell me that I am wrong – was the thought of Wembley. Nobody wanted to miss out and I, for one, was determined not to be injured before 12 May.

On 2 May, I was released to play for Ireland in an important European Championship match against Denmark in Dublin. A 26,000 crowd saw us keep the pressure on England with a

2–0 win, and Frank and I were both pleased to come away with two points . . . and injury-free.

It was a very good omen for us. Because Ireland's Championship hopes were good at that time, and we knew that if we kept close on England's heels we could go to Wembley for the final match of Group One looking for victory . . . and a place in the Rome Finals.

Arsenal's build up for the Wembley date with Manchester United was in total contrast with the anxious build up twelve months previously.

We were relaxed, composed and eagerly looking forward to the actual match. And this is surely the key. Usually when a team reaches Wembley, it is swept along in the whole circus – and often struggles to stay sufficiently detached from all the fuss.

But having gone through the mill only twelve months earlier, we were prepared for the pressure and able to enjoy every minute of the countdown. We learned a lot about the secrets of Cup Final preparation from 1978, including what to expect if we were beaten – and there was no way that was going to happen again.

Only the game itself mattered to us. I even went as far as ignoring all the newspapers, something I wish I had done the year before.

Then, with my injury on my mind, I read articles which predicted disaster for Arsenal if I did not play and became genuinely worried by the 'Brady the key to Arsenal's success' obsession.

After the Ipswich match John Giles contacted me and said how sorry he was he changed his mind about ringing me before the game. He wanted to tell me not to read a single paper, but to relax and prepare myself mentally for the job.

Little did John know that his 'late' advice would prove so useful a year later! Just as he suggested I turned my back on all the rubbish the papers seem convinced they have to publish before a major match.

Just as I felt an ill-wind blowing in our direction before the first Final, I sensed nothing but good vibrations as 12 May approached.

179

The lads were at ease. Big Pat Jennings, already holder of a winners' medal from his days with Spurs and a losers' medal with us in 1978, was calmness itself. So was Pat Rice, no doubt drawing on all the experience he gained from his three previous Finals.

Brian Talbot could not help but get wrapped up in the possibility of helping us to win the trophy he had helped prevent us from winning the last time he was at Wembley. And so it went on – a squad itching to 'go back' and make the most of our second chance.

Terry Neill and Don Howe got the message across. Don said: 'We got beaten here last year and we let an awful lot of people down. This year we are going to make up for that.'

In the opposite camp lay danger. Of that there was no doubt. Even United's manager was the man Arsenal wanted before 'reclaiming' Howe. Dave Sexton had also been through the whole process before . . . and emerged a winner with Chelsea in 1970.

Lads like Sammy McIlroy, Arthur Albiston, Martin Buchan, Steve Coppell . . . all returning to the scene of their 1977 triumph over Liverpool. Big Joe Jordan preparing to give Willie Young a robust and troublesome ninety minutes. Make no mistake, we gave United full credit for their semi-final success over Liverpool and were under no illusions.

I remember comparing my feelings, as we arrived at Wembley on 12 May, with how I had felt just one year earlier. And that comparison in itself gave me a feeling of inner strength.

This time, this time . . . no mistakes this time.

The day was hot and the atmosphere far more intimidating because of the fanatical support for United as well as Arsenal. The Old Trafford fans, like ours, knew the ropes, knew the ground and how to behave on such a very special day.

I suppose the worst part of a Cup Final is the pre-match ceremony and introductions. Really, the players want only one thing after that tense wait down in the cold, semi-soundproof tunnel, and that is to start warming up and getting the feel of the ball.

One member of the Arsenal camp who would not be getting a touch of the ball was the unlucky Malcolm Macdonald. After three Wembley Finals – two with Newcastle United – he had only runners-up medals to show for all the running and goals that those three Cup runs required of him. And now, as we stood on the threshold of triumph, he had to sit it out with Terry, Don and Fred Street on the benches set way back off the pitch.

And on the day he again produced a few quips and words of encouragement while deep down he must have been feeling sick, disappointed and even a little bitter about the way fate dealt him such a cruel blow – a career, with years still beckoning at the top of his profession, lying in ruins because of a knee injury. But even then he did not know that his First Division career had only one game left.

Even on such important days as FA Cup Finals it is a foolish player who does not realize that such a fate could await him after every single game he plays. That is one reason why every game has to be played to the maximum. It just might be the last.

The match got off to a moderate start. United took up the initiative and threw everything into early attacks that certainly had us rocking a bit.

But I was playing deep on the left of the action, close to Sammy Nelson during those early minutes, determined not to become ensnared in any man-to-man marking ploy Sexton may have had prepared for me.

So it was something of an irony that with my first real touch of the ball I managed to weave across the pitch, from left to right, going past three men en route before laying a simple ball square. Frank Stapleton played it into the box, and David Price took up the running, tempting Buchan into an unsuccessful lunge before cutting the ball back from the right goal-line. It says something for the determination in our side that Brian Talbot and Alan Sunderland arrived on the scene at precisely the right moment – and even the television cameras were unable to decide which one of them rammed the ball past Gary Bailey.

Only after the game did Brian get the credit he deserved for giving us the lead.

Back came United, but now they were lofting high balls

181

towards Jordan's head and, although he was a willing battler, Willie matched him, ruining all hopes of a clean knock-down for the waiting Macari and Greenhoff.

As we tuned in to the tempo of the match, our tactics were clearly the more successful. Brian's amazing stamina enabled him to overcome the blistering heat and suffocating cauldron created by the closed-in stadium and 100,000 people. He ran hard, long and unselfishly, hustling United into errors and wrecking one attempted build-up after another.

Our second goal ought to have buried United alive. Frank Stapleton headed in my curling cross from the right of the box, and we all sensed a victory in the air, a complete and impressive victory.

Yet at half-time, Terry and Don did their best to keep feet firmly on the ground, reminding us that we needed to hold onto the initiative and hit more goals. They wanted nothing left to chance. Because at this level, it is fatal to underestimate opponents, no matter what the score. And so it was to prove.

I am sure that I am in the vast majority when I say that I find it hard to recall large slices of the second half. It was as if our two goals had killed the game as a spectacle. Nobody expected United to come back, especially when we did such a good job of shutting them out for the first fifteen minutes after the break.

In that draining heat, our lead must have seemed more and more like a steep hill. But Thomas and Coppell came more into the game as the half wore on. We were guilty of failing to bury them. We certainly had the chances as United pushed more men forward.

I doubt if even Dave Sexton was thinking of anything else other than how to soften the blow as the eighty-sixth minute clicked up on a 100,000 watches. But it was then that the 1979 Cup Final was transformed from a moderate affair into something football supporters will discuss for as long as the game is played.

When the ball was whacked across our area and turned back from the left of the box by Jordan. Gordon McQueen stuck out a telescopic limb and steered a low shot wide of Pat Jennings's left hand. We were angry with ourselves for conceding what we nevertheless saw as nothing more than a late, brave consolation goal.

But something was wrong. We were flagging, sloppy, too sure of a win we had not yet achieved. United, virtually beaten for most of the afternoon, at last saw a glimmer of light. And they went for it like men fresh out of the dressing-room.

I shall never forget that agonizing, slow-motion twisting run of Sammy McIlroy's as he cut into our area, past suddenly weary and frightened yellow shirts, before stroking the coolest of left-foot shots just inside Pat's right hand upright.

Less than two minutes from achieving everything and it seemed as if we had blown it. I remember the awful feeling that we had lost the game. It was 2–2, but to me it seemed as if United were capable of coming straight back into our half and scoring a third. They were out of their skins with excitement . . . and it was their undoing.

Words will never adequately describe how I felt at that moment. I wanted to blame somebody, to get it out of my system, to scream my head off at our collective stupidity. But it had happened so fast that there was nobody to blame. Either that or everybody.

One thought was uppermost in my mind – reach extra time. And as I saw it, the only way of doing that was by keeping possession and taking the ball deep into United's half.

There was no need to communicate this to the rest of the lads. They knew it as well as I did. So I just did what I always try to do when I have the ball, I ran at them. It was vital for those remaining seconds to catch United while they were still mentally celebrating, to push them back towards their own goal, to buy time.

It all seemed so bloody unreal. One minute holding what seemed an untouchable lead. The next hanging on for grim life and battling against your own innermost wish to simply sink down on to the turf.

Like a slow-motion sequence I remember pushing the ball up the inside-left channel, behind the retreating red shirts. It was then that Graham Rix made his marvellous run, calling upon all the concentration and discipline instilled in him by Arsenal and willing his legs to carry him beyond a challenge.

Right up to the moment of defeat I doubt if United realized

the danger. They really thought they had saved the game and must have been convinced that their comeback would see them through extra time.

Graham's beautiful left-foot cross whipped into the goal-mouth where Alan Sunderland, pounding into position, turned it past the stranded, and bewildered, Bailey with his right foot.

There was not enough time left to comprehend what had happened. But I have never known the roar of a crowd switch from one end of a stadium to the other and back again in such dramatic fashion.

God knows I didn't know whether to laugh or cry. It was the most emotional and satisfying moment of my career and, in true fairy-tale fashion, the complete turn-around after the disaster of 1978.

We had won the FA Cup. I had made up for my mistake.

Our dressing-room was just a temporary haven from the heat and exhaustion. Unlike last season, this time we wanted to get back into the sunlight and the limelight. Only by being there and doing it again can you really understand what it is like to play at Wembley and lose and play at Wembley and win.

The moment which said it all for me occurred deep in the bowels of Wembley, in our dressing-room where the champagne flowed and the babble of voices made it impossible to hear who was saying what. Sammy Nelson came over to me and without saying a single word, he showed me his medal and smiled. I picked up mine and did likewise.

We had come through from the Arsenal system, experienced all the changes and rows and worries and fears as the various teams broke up. Now we had something to show for being professional footballers. We were winners, even if we knew that in twenty-four hours we would be considered as defending FA Cup holders and expected to go out and do it all over again.

You are a winner from the moment the final whistle sounds to the time the sun sets. Once that sun rises again you were a winner yesterday. It is time to get back to the business of securing another handful of hours of incomparable joy.

Oddly enough one of my less happy memories of the Final was the stupid and totally unnecessary fuss made over the fact that a few of us swopped shirts with the United players.

It is all very well pompously pointing out the FA rules concerning such things. But all I can say is that the people who make such rules have clearly never played in an FA Cup Final. And if any of them have they have short memories. Do they really believe that any of those players could remember what the FA official told them before the game as they sank to their knees after such a match?

But I suppose that we must accept that there are certain types of people in this world who can never be satisfied . . . the types who if you gave them the world would whine about the fact that it rotates in the wrong direction.

Two good teams from two great clubs met at Wembley on 12 May 1979. One of those teams went home empty-handed yet contributed an exact 50 per cent of the entertainment, excitement and value for money. I knew how they felt, those United players. I knew what it was like to trudge off Wembley's pitch, almost being knocked over by the stampede of photographers and cameramen heading for the winners.

So I swopped my shirt with an opponent. I was not the only one. I cannot see what harm was done by such a gesture. I can only see it as a sporting and genuine mark of respect for a worthy opponent. Such things are difficult to provide for in coldly calculated rule-books.

It was a great day, too, for my family. For Ray and Pat, the ex-professional brothers of mine who never reached an FA Cup Final. For everyone in the family who helped set me on the road to professional football and success.

With the celebrations over, we returned to business on the next Monday night. Our away game at Chelsea was the last of that season. It was also to be the last professional game Malcolm Macdonald would play in the Football League.

It was fitting that he should go out in characteristic fashion – scoring the headed goal that earned us a 1–1 draw.

But as he packed his bags for a summer stint of playing in

Sweden, I packed mine in preparation for Ireland's crucial European Championship match in Bulgaria. And by this time it was becoming difficult to know when one season ended and another began.

17

A Question of Consistency

Inconsistency is the biggest single criticism levelled against referees.

And if only they realized that their inconsistency is also the biggest single cause of trouble between officials and players.

The Football League has some of the best referees in the world. But it also has some of the worst. And it just is not fair to the players, clubs and fans.

The system seems farcical. An amateur holding absolute authority in a professional game. Some of these men are very good at their jobs and make an effort to operate on the same wavelength as the players.

But some of them are absolute mugs, out of touch with what is going on around them, unaware of the tricks of the trade known to virtually every player and more concerned with impressing an assessor than dispensing justice.

It goes without saying that the behaviour of some of my fellow professionals also leaves a lot to be desired, but then you find good and bad in all walks of life.

I have been sent off in the past and deserved to be. But I have also been sent off in a game where my opponent would have been arrested for assault and battery if he had gone for me the way he did in any situation outside football.

The problem now is that players do not know what to expect in given situations. One official will book you for deliberate handball, another will not.

Some referees hammer the tackle from behind, others consider it part and parcel of a physical contact sport. And far too

187

many referees appear to disagree about what constitutes being offside and interfering with play.

I have seen tremendous scoring shots disallowed because a player happened to be standing in an offside position out by a corner flag. What advantage he could be seeking to gain escapes me since usually he is left there by a defender who prefers the easy option of running away from his opponent, his goal and the ball rather than facing up to the man-to-man responsibility.

Yet some officials will allow such a scoring shot to stand on this very basis – that nobody is interfering with play. Either way one of the teams is going to be upset!

We must have set decisions and stick to them. Only then will that large percentage of bookings which result from heat of the moment 'dissent' be avoided.

But the individual referees could do a lot more themselves. Some people advocate that they work and train with professional clubs all the time. That could be the answer, but until it is done on a big scale, nobody is in a position to judge.

Certainly I believe that officials should make a bigger effort to know the players and the different aspects of the pro game. Following the laws and waving plastic, coloured cards around is all very well. But if more referees got inside the game and really understood the little tricks and ploys of the players, the whole situation would change. They would earn a damn sight more respect for a start.

Too many so-called experts pontificate about the behaviour of players and the problems referees have keeping control of games.

What I feel obliged to point out to these people is the very important fact that football is our living – it pays our bills. But it is not the living of the man with the power to stop me from earning mine!

I can give you an example. Arsenal played away to Stoke City on the 23 March 1977. It was a poor time at Highbury and I was far from happy with life anyway. So when Steve Waddington makes it obvious from the kick-off that he has been detailed to mark me tight for ninety minutes, I feel completely cheesed off.

The guy whacked me six times in the opening ten minutes. On the seventh – lucky for some but not for him – my fist laid him out. I'd taken all I was prepared to take.

The referee, quite rightly, sent me off. I was in the wrong and had to go. But he also showed everyone that he knew the cause by booking Waddington. And if he knew the bloody cause, why did he not clamp down on Waddington after the second or third foul? Had he acted at the right time I would not have lost my temper, Waddington would not have been floored and the fans would have seen a proper game instead of the inferior 10 $v.$ 11 scrap that usually results when a team loses a man early on.

I am not very proud of my behaviour that day, but I am convinced it could all have been avoided if the official had seen from the beginning that a 'stop him from playing' instruction had clearly been issued to Waddington. But until referees become more aware of such obvious potential flashpoints, they will continue to tarnish the game.

This is one of the problems every young lad will face – operating on a match-to-match basis as far as officials are concerned. Some will chat to you, share a joke while keeping total control over the match. Others are out there for their own benefit and seem to want to attract more attention than the two teams.

Only experience can teach you how to spot the good from the bad. And it may take you some time to understand how you can be booked for saying something while someone else gets no more than a finger-wagging for chopping some unfortunate player's legs from under him.

It's all down to interpretation, and this brings us back to inconsistency.

One of the worst examples of this that I have ever experienced was at the beginning of the 1978–79 season when Arsenal went on a pre-season European tour.

We played a Bundesliga team, Fortuna Düsseldorf, in a so-called friendly that turned out to be a dummy-run for World War III.

The referee, whose name is impossible even to pronounce, was also German, and for the life of me I cannot understand how or why the whole match went so haywire.

He was aware of what was going on and pulled out the yellow card a couple of times. But the match was getting totally out of hand and the man might as well have been sitting in the bath for all the control he had.

Finally he called the two captains together and warned them that the next bad tackle would be punished with a sending-off.

We were relieved to hear it because some of us were in danger of missing the whole season the way the Germans were tackling.

One minute later I gave the ball to Alan Sunderland . . . and the next thing I knew, Alan was sprawled on the ground, his legs chopped from under him. The referee, standing only a few yards away, waved play on.

I was in the unfortunate position of being the Arsenal player nearest to the situation. I honestly believe that in the heat of that battle any one of the lads would have done the same thing. When the next German came within range, I tackled him the way I'd attempt to stop a Panzer tank.

Out came the red card. He saw that tackle, of course, and satisfied the baying fans by sending me off.

Once again I got what I deserved. But really the whole thing was so unnecessary. The man was not in control of that game and that is why it erupted.

Here, again, a problem arises with foreign officials. The laws of the game are written down for everyone to read and understand. But there are many little 'extras' abroad that drive you up the wall.

In some countries you are not allowed to call for the ball. I have played in games where I have conceded a free kick by calling out the name of a team-mate – yet we are all taught to call for the ball all the time, to provide support for the man in possession.

Getting used to these 'extras' is troublesome, especially in a big game where such a free kick could cost you the match.

Once again it is inconsistency – be it Football League or international, inconsistency is the root of most player-referee problems.

When Arsenal played Magdeburg in the Cup Winners' Cup

second-round, first-leg tie at Highbury on 24 October 1979, David O'Leary was penalized for doing something players do every time they play in British football.

He nipped in between two East Germans and poked the ball away from them by stretching forward his leg. But this is illegal on the Continent where they consider it to be showing studs to an opponent.

We were 1–0 up at the time, and when the whistle went we were stunned. We were even more stunned seconds later when they equalized from the free kick, grabbing a precious away goal in what ended as a 2–1 win for us.

But none of us knew what the free-kick was for until it was explained afterwards. Yet the laws are supposed to be universal.

It is the same problem of interpretation when it comes to what constitutes striking an opponent.

As I mentioned earlier, I was sent off during the UEFA Cup second-round tie in 1978 when Arsenal met Hadjuk Split of Yugoslavia. And this time I was the most astonished person in the stadium.

They detailed a hard-man to follow me wherever I went, and he took his job seriously. He pulled my shirt, kicked the backs of my legs and spat at me now and again just to make sure I knew I was playing in Europe.

But things were made worse because I could sense that the referee was growing tired of the whole situation. He gave me three or four free kicks in as many minutes, but I could tell he was losing his patience – with the defender for his fouls and with me for being the cause of the fouls.

Things came to a head when I tried to escape the clutches of my marker for the umpteenth time and pushed him away with a sweep of my arm. It was not even a foul that I could see, just a case of trying to wrestle myself out of his grasp.

When the referee came over and reached into his pocket I remember feeling relieved because I believed that if he booked the man then I would get a bit of peace for a while. So imagine how I felt when he showed us both the red card.

He honestly interpreted my movement with my arm to be a strike at an opponent. And why he sent off the Yugoslav on that

191

occasion is really beyond me because he had done nothing except get pushed to one side!

The truth was that the referee was sick and tired of both of us and wanted us off the pitch. He did not want to send off one so he solved his problem by getting us out of his way for the rest of the night.

I deliberately avoid naming any of these officials because it is not my intention to blast individuals in a situation where they cannot reply. It is the whole system that is off-beam.

There are extremes of standards, and that is bad. There are too many situations open to varied interpretation. That is also bad. Referees and players are not really on the same wavelength. That is very bad.

Of course there are always exceptions. Gordon Hill was a fine referee, a man who knew what was going on all the time and could never be kidded. If you gave him any lip he gave as good as he got. He understood the pressures and the emotions unleashed during a game. He was respected by players and therefore kept control of the most crucial matches.

Although he did not referee a League game in which I was playing during his career, Jack Taylor always impressed me as being at one with the game and the people in it. He kept things going and often seemed almost invisible – and that is some achievement for a man Jack's height.

Tom Reynolds is a damn good referee because he makes his point early on and will hammer offenders if they step out of line. You know where you stand with him.

Clive Thomas knows what is going on and does understand the players. But I also think he is a bit of a showman and is always prone to making a controversial decision.

One of the youngest referees is Clive White and he impresses me with his efficiency and determination to keep the game moving. He will quickly tell you what's what if you break one of the laws, but often he does it running alongside you, thereby keeping the game going and not humiliating you in front of thousands of fans.

Yes, we do have some top-class officials. But I believe that we need more. The list needs a bit of weeding and new, young officials are required.

Perhaps if it was made more worth their while, referees would come forward. That again is open to debate.

But what is not open to debate is the fact that the modern game is faster than ever before, more demanding, more lucrative, and played more often. It demands a level of consistency from the professionals who play the game.

I say it's time it made the same demands on the men who referee.

18

End of One Era

The question seemed harmless enough. 'Tell us Liam, with one year of your Arsenal contract to run, where do you see your future?' But my reply was to cause more fuss than I could have possibly imagined and lead to months of pressure, rumours and suspicions.

We had just won the FA Cup. Every member of Arsenal Football Club was in a state of understandable excitement. I was no exception . . . apart from the fact that on top of the excitement I also felt a sense of relief.

I had made up my mind to leave the club and try my luck on the Continent even before we reached Wembley. But it was very important to me that I help the club to win a major honour before going.

After spending eight years at Highbury I had only a runners-up medal as the measure of my achievements at club-level. And with so many people building me up as a footballer with something special to offer, I wanted to justify my status and reputation.

Before we played Manchester United I was still haunted by the fact that I had contributed to our failure against Ipswich in the 1978 Final. After we had played United I felt a marvellous sense of release. I knew it was time to announce my intentions.

The club was happy, the squad strong and getting stronger and for the first time in Arsenal's history, they were competing in the European Cup Winners' Cup.

I was, therefore, delighted to give a straight answer to the journalist's question. I told him, and his colleagues, that I was interested in following in the footsteps of Kevin Keegan.

I wanted people to understand that I was not angling for a new and better Arsenal contract. Nor was I saying that I wanted to leave simply for effect.

But if I had honestly known the result of my admission in advance I would have kept my mouth shut.

Perhaps people may think I was naive to suppose that I could simply leave Highbury and sign for a Continental club without anybody being too bothered. But it is not that simple a situation, not for any footballer.

Of course I expected the club to try and keep me in England. I would have been disappointed if they had thought no more of me than that after all those years.

And I considered the supporters. More so than they probably realize. It would be impossible coldly to dismiss them as 'paying customers' as many clubs actually do. To me the Arsenal fans were tremendous – kind, encouraging and appreciative.

They voted me their 'Player of the Year' three times – the third just when such an award became as embarrassing as it was flattering. In fact the more letters I received asking me to stay and the more people who came up and actually pleaded countless damn good reasons why I should stay, the more I began to wish I had said nothing.

I remembered Kevin Keegan's experiences at Liverpool after he had told them that season 1976–77 was going to be his last at Anfield.

By playing fair with his club, Kevin brought a heap of pressure on himself because he had to play through that season in front of a fanatical crowd who gradually began to realize that his was no idle threat, he really was, in their eyes, abandoning them.

Yet as soon as Kenny Dalglish was signed from Celtic and began scoring goals, Keegan was spoken about in the past tense, discussed in the same breath as Ian St John, Roger Hunt and Bill Shankly. Within a matter of weeks he had become part of Liverpool's great history.

What helped him on his way to Hamburg was the fact that Keegan went out with an explosive finish to a great Football

195

League career. He helped Liverpool to win the League Championship, narrowly failed to achieve a League and FA Cup 'double' when Manchester United beat them 2–1 at Wembley and played the game of his life against Borussia Moenchengladbach in Rome as Liverpool became the Champions of Europe.

My modest achievements can hardly be compared with those of Keegan. But it was important to go out with some kind of triumph as a parting shot. That Cup Final win gave me the extra confidence to announce my intentions to Arsenal, and the world.

Keegan always maintained that he could have kept quiet, finished his contract and then told Liverpool that he wanted to play in Europe. By so doing he would have enjoyed a problem-free season up to his departure.

By doing what he believed to be the honourable thing he succeeded in creating a publicity monster of one season's duration.

I did the same thing, and for the same reasons. I believe Keegan's philosophy to be the correct one. It would have been so much easier for me to have said nothing after Wembley. I could have played through season 1979–80 knowing that my contract was nearly up, that I was free to negotiate my own future at the end of the season and yet stay clear of the endless and speculative headlines which attempted to guess my destination.

I was linked with at least ten top clubs, at home and abroad. But it is totally fair to say that hardly any of the rumours had a segment of foundation, and some of the clubs supposedly chasing my signature had not even contacted Arsenal, let alone asked about me.

It is difficult to pinpoint exactly why I wanted to go abroad. Those people who harped on about my leaving only for the money were wrong, very wrong.

As it happens, Arsenal offered me a contract and security which amounted to the best deal I would probably have received anywhere in Great Britain. It was both generous and attractive.

Clearly I rated highly enough to be offered more than any

other player in the club's history.

I considered Arsenal's offer. Who wouldn't? It offered me a lot in terms of security and reasons to stay at Highbury. I could have signed another contract, put my mind at ease and carried on happily in the environment I know best of all – the First Division.

But something inside me ached to step outside the safe borders of England. I wanted a fresh challenge, new surroundings, tougher tests of my capabilities.

If I had really wanted big money and nothing more, I could have signed for one of the top clubs in the United States, lived in a penthouse, swanned around in an open-plan Cadillac, revelled in all the publicity stunts and played a very relaxed type of football on artificial pitches.

But I wanted the very opposite. I look at Keegan and I see a professional who has improved his game all round because of his transfer from Liverpool to Hamburg.

I am a long way from being a complete player. I want to achieve much more as a footballer, develop my game considerably and learn new techniques.

I believed I could achieve all these things on the Continent. Tighter marking, different types of play, new training routines and a new atmosphere, devoid of the familiarity represented by Arsenal.

At Highbury I was one of the star players. I had good friends, lads with whom I had grown up – Graham Rix, Sammy Nelson, Ritchie Powling and the rest of the squad. A warm crowd, who did much to lift me in lean times and backed me totally in success, is something else not to be taken for granted. I knew before a home game that I was going to receive a lot of support from all four corners of the stadium. The Arsenal fans are difficult to please. But when they are behind you, they can be great.

Opting to leave all that behind at twenty-four is not an easy decision, no matter what people may believe.

My family naturally received an equal consideration. We are a close-knit family we Bradys, and putting an extra few thousand miles between me and them was not something I could do just by shrugging my shoulders and

197

saying: 'Yes, but think of the money.'

I know what to expect abroad – loneliness, perhaps initial hostility, a lack of human contact through language difficulties, frustration at what will be a very limited level of communication, days of despair when home will seem to be beckoning across the water, days of utter bewilderment as I learn how to adapt myself to a new team and a new style of football.

Oh yes, it makes a strange and illogical list of reasons for packing up what you know for something you don't know and can only face by anticipating the worst.

If money were the only reason, there are many other ways of earning it without such tough ingredients thrown in.

Tony Woodcock summed up my feelings when he expressed his own shortly before leaving Nottingham Forest to join the West German club Cologne. He said: 'I feel I have to go now because the time is right. If I leave it any longer I may never get the opportunity again.'

That is the often forgotten aspect of this game. You can put off making such a big decision for one year after another. Then, as with Malcolm Macdonald, an injury cuts your career dead and the chance is gone forever. Or your form deteriorates, or football fashions change and nobody bids for you.

I believe that I will become a better player by playing in Europe. I cannot, however guarantee that I will be a success once I leave these shores. And as I have already said, I really cannot hold up my hands and say that I enjoyed my involvement in European competition while with Arsenal.

So there is no magic spell working for me. I have to make this work for myself. Or face the consequences . . . failure.

Nothing will stand between me and my international involvement and I cleared that with John Giles. Just as Cunningham, Keegan and Woodcock went to foreign clubs with the understanding that their England careers would not suffer because of their moves, so I have it assured that Ireland and Liam Brady do not have to part company because I have left Britain for a few years.

It is appropriate that my new life should begin in a new decade. All of the 1970s for me concerned playing in Dublin for

St Kevin's, being spotted by Arsenal, joining the club, working my way up through the various teams, watching a great club going through the slow and agonizing process of change, entering the international arena, playing at Wembley and discovering European competition.

A good and productive decade in which I believe I have learned a lot, made my mistakes and paid for them. In certain cases made up for them. I can only advise every lad who wants to become a professional footballer to heed a few of the advice snippets I have provided.

You must learn from other players. You need advice and guidance, but that does not mean abandoning your right to make your own decisions, to behave like an individual.

Be aware of the fact that you are entering a business as well as a sport. If you are lucky – as I was to join Arsenal – you will begin your career with a good club, a big club which knows how to handle youngsters and get the best out of them – sometimes.

Wherever you end up, do not fall into the trap of believing you are indispensable. You really are only as good as your last game. And if you ever acquire a reputation as a good player you will discover that you are only as good as your next game!

Loyalty, as such, is very rare. Sentimentality belongs mainly in the press and match programmes. What do matter are honesty, as a person and a professional, integrity, self-confidence, hard work, determination, ambition and basic common sense.

Perhaps the best possible example lies with those very supporters who made me their Player of the Year three times.

The moment I announced that I was leaving I sensed a certain change in their attitude towards me. They still saluted achievement and applauded skill. But whereas mistakes were forgiven and forgotten almost immediately when I was a long-term regular and part of the Highbury scenery, as soon as it became apparent that I was preparing to leave, the fans actually began to emit those familiar rumbling, mumbling noises of discontent whenever I made a bad pass or messed up a move.

It was not malicious. It was not barracking. It was not even deliberate. But it was noticeable, a natural reaction from people who found it difficult to understand how the loyalty which they believe really exists between player and club, could be 'betrayed' by me.

But then this is the daft and inevitable side of football. Fans who howl for your head and chant obscene songs about you when you play in front of them as a member of the visiting team will, overnight, hoist banners carrying your name if you sign for their club.

Supporters do not follow players, they follow teams which comprise individuals. And as long as that team does not change too suddenly, as long as no more then one or two familiar faces are sold at any one time, then they will carry on supporting what they believe to be the same team.

In truth, of course, they are supporting the club, not the team. If you look at sides such as Manchester City and Queen's Park Rangers in season 1979–80, you discover that the majority of the players who made up their respective first teams were new signings or lads promoted from the Reserves.

The supporters of both clubs can hardly claim to be supporting the same team. They are really following the same club's nominated eleven for any particular week.

When you dismantle the myth, even to this slight degree, you see how naïve it is to set too much store by nonsense like: 'Always wanted to wear the green and grey hoops of so-and-so.' This is the type of garbage the media put into players' mouths and rarely, if ever, the type of remark a player makes of his own free will.

It is not the colour of the shirts you look at, nor their Cup-fighting history, when you first negotiate your contract and examine what the club has to offer you in terms of a career.

Far more important are the club's prospects, the size of their squad, the calibre of that squad, the facilities, and the contract's contents. Success and achievement are the most important things. But never neglect the business side of your career.

The great danger of this topic is that one stands very close to being accused of cynicism. I am not a cynic. And I do believe that while it is unimportant to consider the old clichés when signing for a club, you can, and usually do, become very attached to that club the longer you stay.

But it is important to be able to separate the emotions. Attachment and affection are fine. But when they slip one gear too far forward and become reliance and debt, you have to act.

Clubs sign you because they want you, because you can do a good job for them, in exchange for which they will pay you over and above a living wage. There ends the debt. It is football, the game you love. It is also business, the basis of your working life.

So when people talk about loyalty, ask yourself if you have played fair and square with your club? If you have given them 100 per cent? If you have been a good pro? If you have honoured your contract? If you can answer yes to these questions, then you are in debt to nobody once your contract has expired.

All of which brings me back to Highbury and season 1979–80.

I faced the season – and my future – with a clear conscience. I knew that my decision would bring with it certain problems. But I was determined to give my best to the club up to the last game. And more than that, I began to imagine leaving under similar circumstances to those under which Keegan left Liverpool . . . with a European trophy winner's medal.

The European Cup Winners' Cup was more inviting than the UEFA Cup because it contained more sides capable of the unpredictable – by virtue of their very national Cup triumph – and there is one round less than in the UEFA Cup!

But the most immediate thing was Ireland's important European Championship match in Bulgaria. We knew that two points from this game would really maintain the pressure on England. But as things turned out, we lost the match and a key player with a broken leg.

On 19 May we began against a flagging Bulgaria as if we were going to command the game. But we failed to turn our superiority into goals and our game slowly deteriorated.

In the end they pipped us by a single, second-half goal by Tsvetkov. But the really disturbing thing was the way Jimmy Holmes broke a leg during the game, went to a local hospital and received far from satisfactory treatment.

They put the plaster on his leg too tightly, and by the time we were en route for home, Jimmy was in agony. Luckily the Irish team doctor was at hand and he insisted that we stop off at

201

Geneva and put Jimmy in hospital.

Clearly, Eastern bloc hospital treatment is different from what we are used to. Jimmy was fortunate. It was the opinion of the Swiss doctor that if that plaster had stayed on longer, Jimmy's career would have been threatened.

I suppose we knew then that we had blown another chance of qualifying for a major international tournament. Realistically, England were always the favourites. But it seemed so stupid to slip up against one of the worst sides in the group.

West Germany played us in Dublin three days later, and I suppose national disappointment at our result in Bulgaria was reflected in the 20,000 crowd.

We were level at the interval thanks to a Gerry Ryan goal. But the Germans finished the stronger side, and ran out 3–1 winners.

29 May was a special day for Irish international football. World Champions Argentina arrived in style and John Giles announced that he was making his final appearance in the Irish team.

Of their famous World Cup side, Argentina fielded Fillol, Tarantini, Olguin, Houseman and Valencia. We were also treated to a substitute appearance by Maradona, and although the game finished 0–0, I enjoyed it immensely, especially in the light of the Argentinians' results during their European tour overall.

They beat Holland in a repeat of the World Cup Final, played in Switzerland; drew 2–2 in Italy and hammered Scotland 3–1 at Hampden Park. I reckon our draw was a highly creditable result. So did the Irish supporters.

My summer break involved seeing my family for a spell and, as you may imagine, we discussed my intention to leave Arsenal quite a lot. Not that anybody had it in their mind to try and change mine. I was adamant.

Arsenal began their season back at Wembley. We played Liverpool in the FA Charity Shield match and took a beating. They were superb on the day, showing all the team-work and cohesion and excellent finishing of a great team.

McDermott (2) and Dalglish scored for Liverpool before Alan Sunderland hit a late consolation goal to give the Arsenal contingent in the 92,000 crowd something to cheer.

But that game said a lot about the way the season was to unfold. Liverpool showed in that one game just how good they were and how difficult it was to consider them as anything other than Championship material.

We knew what we had to achieve to reach their standards. Sometimes we did emulate Liverpool's form. But their secret is consistency. And that, especially when it came to scoring goals, we could not achieve.

Yet in their opening match of the League season Liverpool surprisingly dropped a home point in a 0–0 draw with Bolton while we trounced Alan Mullery's newly promoted Brighton, 4–0, at The Goldstone Ground.

I have to say that we were a class above them on the day. And we could and should have scored more.

But in our next two home games we lost 2–0 to Ipswich and drew a dreary match 0–0 with Manchester United. Already our strike-force was erratic. Then we were drawn away to Leeds United in the League Cup's second round, first leg. A goal by Frank Stapleton earned a 1–1 draw, then we went back to Elland Road for a League game and this time Sammy Nelson grabbed a point and a draw with a second-half goal.

But on Tuesday, 4 September, we stunned Leeds – and football – by crushing them 7–0 in the League Cup second round, second leg. Alan Sunderland scored a hat-trick and I scored twice from the spot to make it three penalties out of three.

Terry Neill showed traces of his old habits after what was, admittedly, a poor performance on our part. Two goals up at half-time, we lost 3–2 to a Derby team who began the day looking for their first win of the season! Terry told reporters that he believed some of his players 'needed their backsides kicked'.

However, once again, he made no reference to kicking anyone, anywhere, when he came face to face with his players.

Ireland lost a friendly international 2–1 to Wales, played at Swansea, and it was difficult not to wonder at how everyone in the Irish squad would have been feeling – and might have done against West Germany and Argentina and Wales – if we had taken something home from Bulgaria apart from a badly injured Jimmy Holmes.

England beat Denmark 1–0 at Wembley on 12 September and I remember being very aware of the fact that nothing was going to stop them reaching Rome. It was as if their games against Northern Ireland, Bulgaria and us were meaningless.

Everyone at Highbury threw their glances in the direction of the ceiling when we heard the Cup Winners' Cup draw. Once again we were paired with one of Europe's great glamour clubs . . . Fenerbahce of Turkey!

But they had to be handled properly and beaten. And so they were, 2–0 at Highbury on 19 September. We asked the fans to be patient and they were great. For a long while it looked as if we would have to travel to Turkey for the second leg guarding a slender one-goal lead thanks to Alan Sunderland. But big Willie Young repeated his favourite European party trick by grabbing a second goal just when the Turks thought they had achieved something.

Unfortunately, the very mention of the word Europe any-where near my name was enough to spark off the newshounds. Would I consider the USA? What about Spain? Surely West Germany is the place, just look at Keegan? Will I wait for the rich Italians to end their ban on foreign players after the 1980 European Championships?

The questions were non-stop. And when the answers were not forthcoming, I swear some reporters just made up their own minds and wrote a story based on their own guesswork.

Meanwhile we kept the League Cup in our sights by beating Southampton 2–1 at Highbury in the third round and I scored my fourth goal of the season.

We travelled to Turkey on 3 October where, despite the fanatical atmosphere stoked up by the fans, we fought out a hard-earned 0–0 draw and went through to the second round on a 2–0 aggregate. Once again we crossed fingers, hoping for one of Europe's aristocrats in the next round.

We could have drawn Juventus or Nantes or Valencia. But no, we had to draw yet another team from behind the Iron Cur-tain, this time Magdeburg of East Germany.

Ireland's European Championship hopes, however slender, were maintained when we whipped the mediocre Bulgarians 3–0 in Dublin on 17 October. But the news that England had hammered Northern Ireland 5–1 in Belfast delighted absolutely none of us.

Once again the tragic stupidity of it all was rammed home to us. Two Irish teams doing so well in a group, yet destined to wreck each other's chances.

Arsenal's results were largely 0–0 draws and very disappointing for those people who really believed that we were Championship material. Needless to say, we were not, certainly not in comparison with Liverpool nor Manchester United. I believe one of our biggest problems, and it has been so for years at Highbury, was lack of top-class cover.

We lacked a strong Reserve pool, strength in depth, and this, over the long hard English season, is a must.

However, Magdeburg arrived at Highbury on 24 October, and although they did not excite us in prospect, they gave us a very difficult time and we only managed a 2–1 win, Willie Young scoring another European goal of priceless value to his side.

Ireland played a friendly international against the United States in Dublin, a match which attracted 20,000 people. Perhaps they expected a goal-glut. Whatever they expected, they went home relieved as Ireland clawed back from the brink of a shock defeat to beat the plucky Americans 3–2.

In fairness it was an Irish team of mixed strength. None of the Arsenal lads could play because we had a League Cup fourth round tie away to Brighton which, as seemed in fashion at the time, ended 0–0.

As we had with Leeds, we faced Brighton in the League a few days later and this time won 3–0. But our League Cup date had to wait. It was East Germany next stop . . . and the first concrete hint for me that Arsenal were no longer interested in making a go of keeping me.

Before we left for the second leg of that Cup Winners' Cup tie, the Arsenal Board met, and I have no doubt whatsoever that the situation concerning my contract, and my desire to leave the club, was discussed.

I half expected what followed. But when Terry Neill did approach me on the flight across Europe, I was a little disappointed.

205

He made the obvious observation that, if I decided to leave Arsenal before my contract expired, the club would benefit from a sizeable transfer fee and I could virtually take my pick of the offers.

I should stress that nobody was trying to push me out. That would be very unfair to imply. But there is no doubt that the hint was deliberately dropped. I was set on leaving, then why wait until my contract was up? Why not get things going?

One very good reason – once my contract expired I became a free agent and in a position to negotiate my own contract, with the help of my solicitor.

I still said nothing in the press and concentrated only on my football. And I got on the score-sheet in our 2–2 draw in East Germany, a result which put us in the quarter-finals on a 4–3 aggregate.

Poor Brighton took another drubbing off us in that League Cup replay – 4–0 at Highbury, and it was a match which marked the arrival of an impressive young striker, Paul Vaessen, who scored two fine goals.

And so the production line continues. It seemed only a matter of months earlier that I had stepped on to the pitch as substitute against Birmingham City and walked off feeling ten feet tall.

Paul Vaessen will no doubt go through the same ups and downs, face the same crossroads in his career, experience the same eye-openers along the way. I wish him well.

For me, Ireland's second meeting with Northern Ireland, in Belfast, turned out to be an anti-climax.

I injured my ankle playing against Everton at Highbury and ironically it was a tackle by my former team-mate Trevor Ross which kept me out of the Irish side beaten 1–0 at Windsor Park on 21 November.

So the North became the first victors from the first two meetings of the Irish international teams. The goal, scored by Gerry Armstrong, will no doubt go down in history and crop up in many a future football quiz.

As I stepped into the 1980s with Arsenal I did so in a strange position, that of a long-serving player, and one of the team's senior members, dedicated to the job of winning another major honour for the club; and professional footballer and individual, determined to make this my last season in the First Division for a few years to come.

As I said before, I also wanted to end my Arsenal career on a winning note. So when the League Cup fifth round draw paired us at home with Third Division Swindon Town, we really believed that we had one foot firmly in the semi-final.

It is hardly an original suggestion that cup competitions regularly produce surprise results. But our tie with Swindon turned out to be a typical cup game. Alan Sunderland put us ahead with an early penalty and we created and missed a number of good chances.

Swindon slowly settled down, kept us out and began to turn the tide. And when Billy Tucker scored their late equalizer we were angry with ourselves, yet still confident that we would not make the same mistake in the replay.

We did worse than that, we lost 4–3 in a tremendous match. I believe we should have gone to a third game, despite making mistakes in defence. But take nothing away from Swindon who went on to reach the semi-finals before losing 4–3 on aggregate to Wolves.

I was troubled by an ankle injury around the start of the New Year, a very frustrating experience, especially as I wanted to keep up my form. Meanwhile Arsenal maintained their Championship challenge, although our home form was not as good as it could have been.

We entered the new decade third in the First Division after a 1–0 win away to Southampton. Then the FA Cup took us down to Cardiff for a 0–0 third round draw. Two Alan Sunderland goals saw us through the replay. Brighton, cup rivals yet again, were beaten 2–0 in the fourth round at Highbury. But for me, the individual highlight of my career was still around the corner.

On Wednesday, 6 February 1980 I captained Ireland, against England, at Wembley. It may seem easy to describe how proud I was that night, but it is not. Nothing else that I have achieved as a professional player can compare with leading my country.

More than 90,000 people saw our final European Championship fixture. They also saw two Kevin Keegan goals beat us for the first time in three international meetings.

I believe we were enjoying more of the play just before each of England's goals. But that is not important now. What does matter is how massive a stride Ireland has taken at international level and how excited we all feel about the World Cup qualifying matches to come.

Personally I find it fitting to end this book as I began it, on an international note. I guess my 'career' began with my being expelled for captaining the Irish Schoolboys, and a decade on, I was again honoured with the captaincy, only this time somewhat higher up the scale.

The result was disappointing. But we let nobody down and I doubt if I will every forget how I felt as we lined up before the match. Like the drowning man, a hell of a lot of my life flashed before me. So much already experienced and so much to try and attain.

A glance in the mirror, a quick check on what ten years of football had done to me and a brief recap of my career to date produced a mixed bag of results. But I have been fortunate, I have been helped along the way by great players, I have been given support from many areas and I believe that I have learned many lessons, some the hard way.

I have to say that, as my new career unfolds, it is very much a case of so far, so good.

Index

209